COPYRIGHT

SPECIAL SALES

For more information about buying this eBook in bulk quantities, or for special sales opportunities (which may include custom cover designs, and content particular to your business or training goals), please send us an email to support@myexcelonline.com

MYEXCELONLINE ACADEMY COURSE

We are offering you access to our online Excel membership course – The MyExcelOnline Academy – **for only $1 for the first 30 days!**

Copy & Paste this $1 Trial URL to your web browser to get access to this special reader offer: https://www.myexcelonline.com/$1trial

CONNECT WITH US

Website, blog & podcast: https://www.myexcelonline.com/

iPhone App: https://www.myexcelonline.com/iphone

Android App: https://www.myexcelonline.com/android

Email: support@myexcelonline.com

AUTHOR BIOGRAPHY

John Michaloudis is the *Founder* and Chief *Inspirational Officer* of MyExcelOnline.com.

John is currently living in the North of Spain, is married and has two beautiful kids. John holds a Bachelor's degree in Commerce (Major in Accounting) and speaks English/Australian, Greek and Spanish.

John decided to leave the "Corporate World" - during his 15 year professional stint as an Accountant & Financial Controller in Avon & General Electric - and start MyExcelOnline, where he could teach the rest of the world on a much grander scale how to use Excel effectively via his blog tutorials, podcast shows, webinar trainings and online courses!

Bryan Hong is a contributor at MyExcelOnline.com. He is currently living in the Philippines and is married to his wonderful wife Esther. Bryan is also a Microsoft Certified Systems Engineer with over 10 years of IT and teaching experience!

TABLE OF CONTENTS

GETTING STARTED

Downloadable Practice Workbooks

Macros are one of the most powerful features in Excel and learning how & when to use them will make you into an Excel superstar!

There are 101 ready-to-use Macros in this book for you to become more efficient at Excel!

To get the most value out of this book, we recommend that you follow our easy to use step by step guide in each Macro.

Download the Workbooks that pertains to each Macro and practice with the Macro by running it on the sample data provided.

Each Macro tutorial has 2 workbooks which you have access to:

1. **"No Code"** - You need to copy & paste the VBA code provided in this book to the VBA Editor and Run the Macro; and
2. **"With Code"** –You need to simply Run the Macro.

For the **download link** that has all the workbooks covered in this book, please go to the **last page of the book**.

Why VBA?

Do you repeat various Excel actions like copy & pasting data, formatting, hiding and unhiding worksheets, to name a few?

Did you know that you can automate your tasks in Excel with a couple of mouse clicks?

If you keep on repeating the same thing over and over again, creating an Excel VBA Macro is perfect for you! It saves you time so you can do things that you like doing, like going home early!

VBA stands for **Visual Basic for Applications**. Visual Basic (VB) is a programming language from Microsoft used to create your own custom applications.

VBA on the other hand, is a smaller version of VB that is included in each Microsoft Office application, **Excel being one of them**. With VBA, you do not need to pay somebody to custom program for your additional functionalities that you need in Excel. You can create your own by combining VBA and Excel!

A common scenario is when you take 30 minutes each day to prepare and format a report. You can use VBA Macros to reduce this work to a single button click! The time savings just stack up and your boss will be impressed with your efficiency.

Not satisfied with the coverage of Excel functions? You can create your own Excel user-defined function using VBA. You can then repeatedly use your user-defined function in the spreadsheet.

Read on and enjoy what the world of VBA has to offer.

How to Use Macros

The 101 Macros in this book simply need to be copied to the VBA Editor and you will be able to use them immediately. When the Macro can be further modified to fit your needs or to expand its capabilities, we will explain how to in this guide.

A Macro is also called a Procedure.

If this is your first time using a Macro, read the introductory section here so that you will be more comfortable with the various Macro lingo.

Here are a few of the most common Macro concepts:

Variables:

We use variables a lot in our code. Variables are containers of your data that is represented by a name you specify. In other words, they are a great way to store and manipulate data.

Loops:

Looping is one of the most crucial programming techniques. It allows us to repetitively do something with just a few lines of code.

Code Comments:

Any line that is **preceded by an apostrophe** ' - turns into a green line of code in the Visual Basic Editor window.

This line is ignored in the code and is used to "document" the code so that it is easier for you/others to understand what the code does.

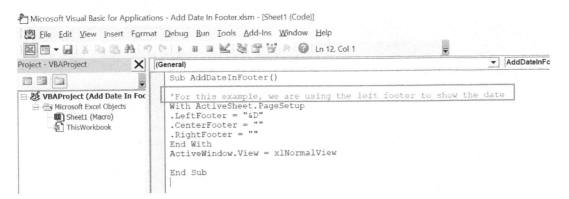

Backup your files!

Before using any of the Macros in your Excel files, a best practice is to back up the Excel file first. This is to provide a safety net if data gets modified in a different way than you expect. You can safely test the Macro this way with your current data and load the previous file if unintended changes take place.

These are the common terms when using Macros:

- **Code** – this is the VBA text

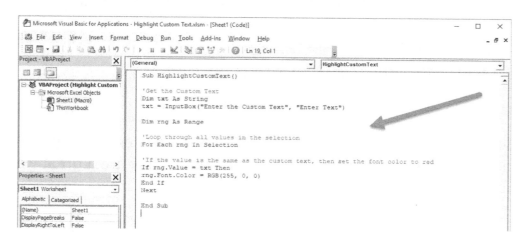

- **Visual Basic Editor** – this is the window where we write/paste our VBA code in. You can get to this window by going to ***Developer > Code > Visual Basic*** or shortcut ***ALT+F11***

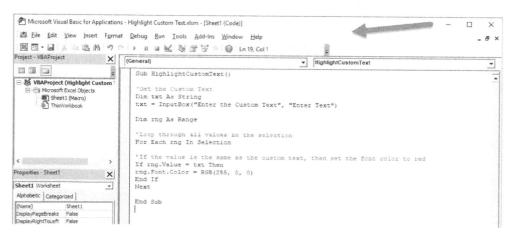

- **Procedures** – these are also called Macros and serve as the containers of our code. Notice that there are no spaces in the procedure name: ***AddDateInFooter()***

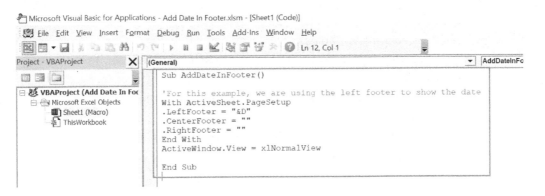

- **Modules** – these are containers of the Procedures

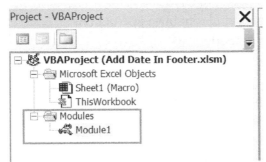

Project – this is a container of Modules. A single Excel workbook is a project of VBA code

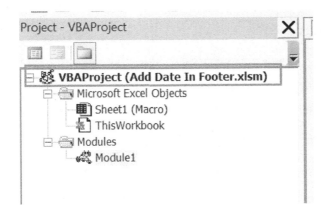

Here is a list of common keywords you will see in Macros. You can always refer back to this list as you go through the examples in the book:

Keyword	Definition
as	Used when defining the data type of a variable
dim	Used for declaring variables
each	Combined with the For keyword (e.g. "for each...") to access the individual components in a collection
else	Combined with the then keyword for alternate scenarios
end	Used to end a procedure
exit	Used to leave a procedure prior to the end statement
for	Used to iterate one or more actions a specific number of times
function	Defines a block of code that can return a value
if	Used for specifying conditions
integer	Used to define a number between -32,768 and 32,767
is	Compares two object references
long	Used to define a number between -2,147,483,648 and 2,147,486,647
next	Used with the For keyword to create set of repetitive instructions
on error	Used to capture and handle errors properly
resume	Used with the On Error keyword to handle errors properly
string	Used to define text variables
sub	Defines a block of code that does not return a value
then	Combined with the If keyword for alternate scenarios
to	Used with the For keyword when repeating
with	Used to perform multiple operations on a single object

Running a Macro

Running a Macro is very straightforward:

Go to **Developer > Code > Macros**

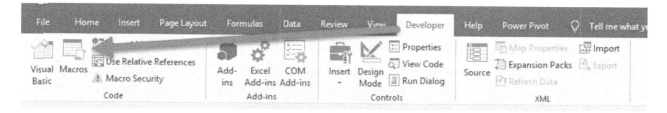

Macros can be located in:

- This Workbook; or
- All Open Workbooks

Make sure your Macro name is selected from the list. Click **Run**.

Then your code will execute from there.

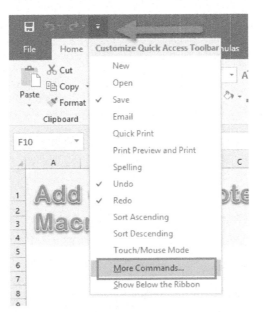

Using the Quick Access Toolbar to run a Macro

If you use a specific Macro frequently, then it is a good idea to add it to the *Quick Access Toolbar* in Excel for easy access.

Go to **Customize Quick Access Toolbar Dropdown > More Commands**

Under the *Choose commands from* drop down, make sure to select *Macros.*
Pick your Macro and click *Add.*

Your Macro should now be added to the Toolbar. Click *OK.*

Click on the Macro icon that is now located on the top or bottom of your Ribbon and it will now run this Macro!

Enabling VBA in Excel

Most Excel workbooks do not have the *Developer* tab activated.

This is needed in order to execute & create Macros. We can easily enable it in a few steps! Make sure you have Excel open...

STEP 1: Right click anywhere on your Ribbon and select *Customize the Ribbon*:

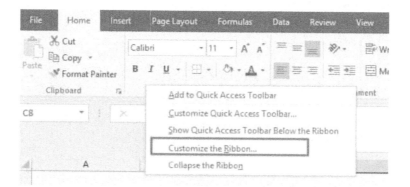

STEP 2: Make sure the **Customize Ribbon** is selected. Then select the **Developer** option under **Main Tabs**. Click **OK.**

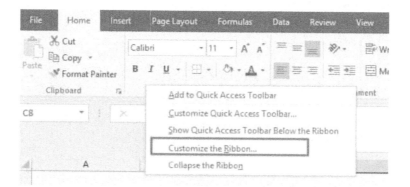

After that you should be able to see the **Developer** tab enabled:

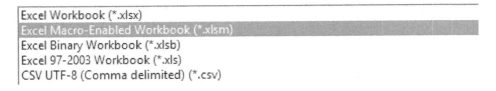

.XLSX vs .XLSM

For a Macro to run, the Workbook's file extension should be in a **.xlsm** format – which is a Macro enabled format.

You can change this under:

File > Save As > Save As Type > Excel Macro-Enabled Workbook(*.xlsm)

Excel Workbook (*.xlsx)
Excel Macro-Enabled Workbook (*.xlsm)
Excel Binary Workbook (*.xlsb)
Excel 97-2003 Workbook (*.xls)
CSV UTF-8 (Comma delimited) (*.csv)

Enabling All Macros

To ensure all Macros in this book will run without any issues, go to *File > Options > Trust Center > Trust Center Settings > Macro Settings*

Ensure **Enable all macros** is selected. Click **OK.**

Insert Button to Run a Macro

What does it do?

We can insert a button and configure it to run a specific Macro. It makes things simpler and the user only needs to click this button every time they want to execute the Macro.

We will be using the **Autofit Columns** Macro Workbook to demonstrate how to create our own button.

The Macro will autofit all of the columns to fit to its contents.

You can use this technique to create buttons to run any Macro.

Final Result:

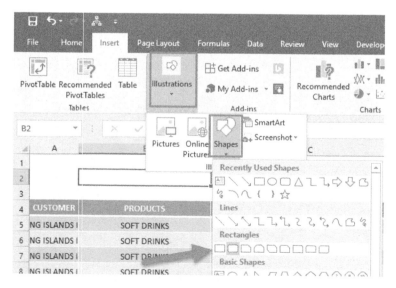

STEP 1: Let us select a shape you prefer. Go to *Insert > Illustrations > Shapes > Rounded Rectangle*:

STEP 2: Place the shape anywhere on the sheet that you want.

Double click on the shape to type the text: **Autofit All Columns**.

You can change the font, font size, and center the text as well.

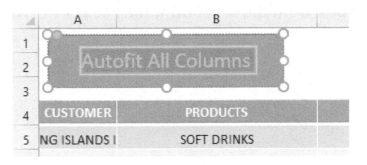

STEP 3: Right click on your shape and select *Assign Macro*

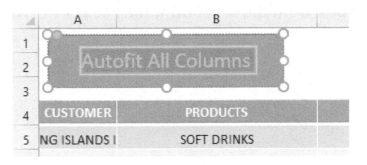

STEP 4: We have one Macro that is already created for you.

Do not worry as we will discuss the <u>Auto Fit All Columns Macro</u> later in the book.

Select **This Workbook** from the dropdown, then select the **AutoFitAllColumns** Macro. Click **OK.**

Let us try it out now! Click on your shape/button and see the magic happen! All of your columns are now autofitted!

	CUSTOMER	PRODUCTS	SALES PERSON	SALES REGION	ORDER DATE	SALES	FINANCIAL YEAR	SALES MONTH	SALES QTR	CHANNEL PARTNERS
5	LONG ISLANDS INC	SOFT DRINKS	Michael Jackson	AMERICAS	4/13/2012	24,640	2012	January	Q1	Acme, inc.
6	LONG ISLANDS INC	SOFT DRINKS	Michael Jackson	AMERICAS	12/21/2012	24,640	2012	February	Q1	Widget Corp
7	LONG ISLANDS INC	SOFT DRINKS	Michael Jackson	AMERICAS	12/24/2012	29,923	2012	March	Q1	123 Warehousing
8	LONG ISLANDS INC	SOFT DRINKS	Michael Jackson	AMERICAS	12/24/2012	66,901	2012	April	Q2	Demo Company
9	LONG ISLANDS INC	SOFT DRINKS	Michael Jackson	AMERICAS	12/29/2012	63,116	2012	May	Q2	Smith and Co.
10	LONG ISLANDS INC	SOFT DRINKS	Michael Jackson	AMERICAS	6/28/2012	38,281	2012	June	Q2	Foo Bars
11	LONG ISLANDS INC	SOFT DRINKS	Michael Jackson	AMERICAS	6/28/2012	57,650	2012	July	Q3	ABC Telecom
12	LONG ISLANDS INC	SOFT DRINKS	Michael Jackson	AMERICAS	6/29/2012	90,967	2012	August	Q3	Fake Brothers
13	LONG ISLANDS INC	SOFT DRINKS	Michael Jackson	AMERICAS	6/29/2012	11,910	2012	September	Q3	QWERTY Logistics
14	LONG ISLANDS INC	SOFT DRINKS	Michael Jackson	AMERICAS	7/6/2012	59,531	2012	October	Q4	Demo, inc.
15	LONG ISLANDS INC	SOFT DRINKS	Michael Jackson	AMERICAS	7/6/2012	88,297	2012	November	Q4	Sample Company
16	LONG ISLANDS INC	SOFT DRINKS	Michael Jackson	AMERICAS	9/8/2012	87,868	2012	December	Q4	Sample, inc
17	LONG ISLANDS INC	BOTTLES	Michael Jackson	AMERICAS	9/8/2012	95,527	2012	January	Q1	Acme Corp
18	LONG ISLANDS INC	BOTTLES	Michael Jackson	AMERICAS	6/30/2012	90,599	2012	February	Q1	Allied Biscuit
19	LONG ISLANDS INC	BOTTLES	Michael Jackson	AMERICAS	12/23/2012	17,030	2012	March	Q1	Ankh-Sto Associates

BASIC MACROS

Add Custom Footer

What does it do?

Adds a custom footer with your text

Copy Source Code:

```
Sub AddCustomFooter()

Dim inputText As String
inputText = InputBox("Enter your text for the custom footer",
"Custom Footer")
'Add your custom text to the right footer
With ActiveSheet.PageSetup
.LeftFooter = ""
.CenterFooter = ""
.RightFooter = inputText
End With
End Sub
```

Final Result:

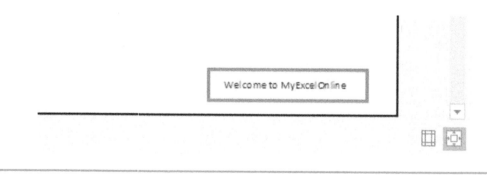

Ever wanted to add a footer to your Excel spreadsheet? You can add a **custom footer** using Excel Macros!

STEP 1: Go to *Developer > Code > Visual Basic*

STEP 2: Paste in your code and **Select Save**. Close the window afterwards.

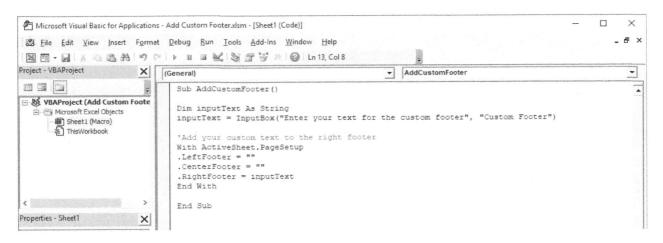

STEP 3: Let us test it out!

Go to *Developer > Code > Macros*

Make sure your Macro is selected. Click **Run**.

STEP 4: Type in your custom footer, **click OK**.

To check if the footer did get added, go to *File > Print*:

Now you should be able to see your text on your footer!

Add Custom Header

What does it do?

Adds a custom header with your text

Copy Source Code:

```
Sub AddCustomHeader()

Dim inputText As String
inputText = InputBox("Enter your text for the custom header",
"Custom Header")
'Add your custom text to the center header
With ActiveSheet.PageSetup
.LeftHeader = ""
.CenterHeader = inputText
.RightHeader = ""
End With
End Sub
```

Final Result:

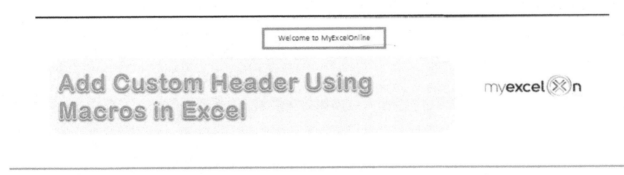

Ever wanted to add a header to your Excel spreadsheet? You can add a **custom header** using Excel Macros!

STEP 1: Go to *Developer > Code > Visual Basic*

STEP 2: Paste in your code and **Select Save**. Close the window afterwards.

STEP 3: Let us test it out!

Go to *Developer > Code > Macros*

Make sure your Macro is selected. Click **Run**.

STEP 4: Type in your custom header, **click OK**.

Custom Header   ×

Enter your text for the custom header | OK |
                                               | Cancel |

| Welcome to MyExcelOnline

To check if the header did get added, go to *File > Print*:

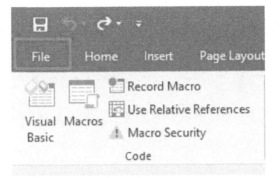

Now you should be able to see your text on your header!

Add Custom Header.xlsm - Excel   Sign in ? — □ ×

Print

Info
New   Copies: 1
Open
Save   Print   Welcome to MyExcelOnline
Save As
             Printer   Add Custom Header Using   myexcel⊗n
Print   HP Photosmart Ink Adv...   Macros in Excel
Share   Offline
Export   Printer Properties
Publish   Settings
Close   Print Active Sheets
                    Only print the active she...
Account   Pages: to
Feedback   Print One Sided
                    Only print on one side of...
                    Collated
                    1,2,3 1,2,3 1,2,3
                    Landscape Orientation

Add Date In Footer

What does it do?

Add the current date to the footer

Copy Source Code:

```
Sub AddDateInFooter()

'For this example, we are using the left footer to show the date
With ActiveSheet.PageSetup
.LeftFooter = "&D"
.CenterFooter = ""
.RightFooter = ""
End With
ActiveWindow.View = xlNormalView

End Sub
```

Final Result:

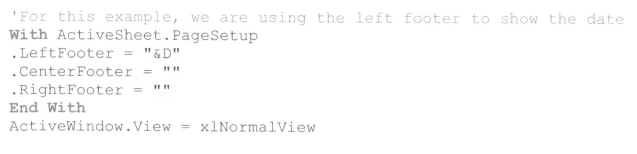

3/20/2019

Adding the current date in the footer is very easy using Excel Macros! You can customize the text even as you see fit if prefer something else instead of the current date.

STEP 1: Go to ***Developer > Code > Visual Basic***

STEP 2: Paste in your code and **Select Save**. Close the window afterwards.

```vba
Sub AddDateInFooter()

'For this example, we are using the left footer to show the date
With ActiveSheet.PageSetup
.LeftFooter = "&D"
.CenterFooter = ""
.RightFooter = ""
End With
ActiveWindow.View = xlNormalView

End Sub
```

STEP 3: Let us test it out!

Go to **Developer > Code > Macros**

Make sure your Macro is selected. Click **Run**.

To check if the header did get added, go to *File > Print*:

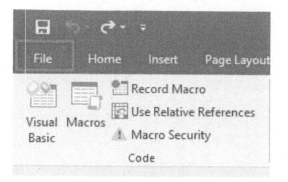

Now you should be able to see the current date on your footer!

Add Date In Header

What does it do?

Add the current date to the header

Copy Source Code:

```
Sub AddDateInHeader()

'For this example, we are using the center header to show the
date
With ActiveSheet.PageSetup
.LeftHeader = ""
.CenterHeader = "&D"
.RightHeader = ""
End With
ActiveWindow.View = xlNormalView

End Sub
```

Final Result:

Did you know that you can **add the current date in header** in Excel? You can add this via Excel Macros in a single click!

STEP 1: Go to *Developer > Code > Visual Basic*

STEP 2: Paste in your code and **Select Save**. Close the window afterwards.

STEP 3: Let us test it out!

Go to *Developer > Code > Macros*

Make sure your Macro is selected. Click **Run**.

To check if the header did get added, go to **File > Print**:

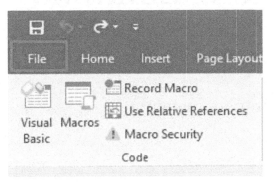

Now you should be able to see the current date on your header!

How to Autofit Columns

What does it do?

Autofit all columns to fit to its contents

Copy Source Code:

```
Sub AutoFitAllColumns()
Activate
Cells.Select

'See the magic happen!
Cells.EntireColumn.AutoFit
End Sub
```

Final Result:

My column widths are all over the place and I want to make it look more presentable. Did you know you can **autofit columns using Macros in Excel?**

And with this cool trick, it can be done in just **one click!**

STEP 1: Go to *Developer > Code > Visual Basic*

STEP 2: Make sure **Sheet2** is selected as we want to autofit the columns there because that's the tab where the data table is stored.

Paste in your code and **Select Save**. Close the window afterwards.

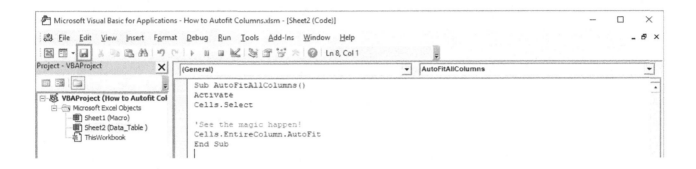

STEP 3: Let us test it out!

Open the sheet containing the data. Go to ***Developer > Code > Macros***

Make sure your Macro is selected. Click **Run**.

With just one click, all of the columns are automatically fitted now!

How to Autofit Rows

What does it do?

Autofit all rows to fit to its contents

Copy Source Code:

```
Sub AutoFitAllRows()
Activate
Cells.Select

'See the magic happen!
Cells.EntireRow.AutoFit
End Sub
```

Final Result:

My row heights are all over the place and I want to make it look more presentable. Instead of adjusting them one by one, did you know you can **autofit rows using Macros in Excel?**

And with this cool trick, it can be done in just **one click!**

STEP 1: Go to *Developer > Code > Visual Basic*

STEP 2: Make sure **Sheet2** is selected as we want to autofit the rows there.

Paste in your code and **Select Save**. Close the window afterwards.

STEP 3: Let us test it out!

Open the sheet containing the data. Go to *Developer > Code > Macros*

Make sure your Macro is selected. Click **Run**.

With just one click, all of the rows are automatically fitted now!

How to Insert Multiple Columns

What does it do?

Asks for a number of columns, then inserts it to the right of your selected cell

Copy Source Code:

```vba
Sub InsertMultipleColumns()

Dim numColumns As Integer
Dim counter As Integer

'Select the current column
ActiveCell.EntireColumn.Select
On Error GoTo Last
numColumns = InputBox("Enter number of columns to insert",
"Insert Columns")

'Keep on insert columns until we reach the desired number
For counter = 1 To numColumns
Selection.Insert Shift:=xlToRight,
CopyOrigin:=xlFormatFromRightorAbove
Next counter
Last: Exit Sub
End Sub
```

Final Result:

	A	B	C	D	E	F
1	CUSTOMER	Column3	Column2	Column1	PRODUCTS	SALES PERSON
2	LONG ISLANDS INC				SOFT DRINKS	Michael Jackson
3	LONG ISLANDS INC				SOFT DRINKS	Michael Jackson
4	LONG ISLANDS INC				SOFT DRINKS	Michael Jackson
5	LONG ISLANDS INC				SOFT DRINKS	Michael Jackson
6	LONG ISLANDS INC				SOFT DRINKS	Michael Jackson
7	LONG ISLANDS INC				SOFT DRINKS	Michael Jackson
8	LONG ISLANDS INC				SOFT DRINKS	Michael Jackson
9	LONG ISLANDS INC				SOFT DRINKS	Michael Jackson
10	LONG ISLANDS INC				SOFT DRINKS	Michael Jackson

Ever wanted to try to **insert multiple columns** just by typing in a number? It is possible using Macros in Excel!

Plus you also get to learn some programming tricks along the way, how cool is that?

STEP 1: Go to **Developer > Code > Visual Basic**

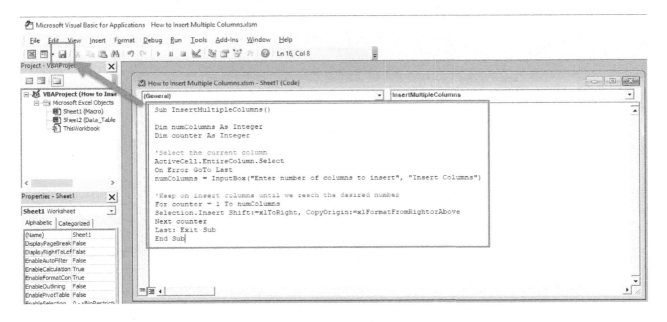

STEP 2: Paste in your code and **Select Save**. Close the window afterwards.

```
Sub InsertMultipleColumns()

Dim numColumns As Integer
Dim counter As Integer

'Select the current column
ActiveCell.EntireColumn.Select
On Error GoTo Last
numColumns = InputBox("Enter number of columns to insert", "Insert Columns")

'Keep on insert columns until we reach the desired number
For counter = 1 To numColumns
Selection.Insert Shift:=xlToRight, CopyOrigin:=xlFormatFromRightorAbove
Next counter
Last: Exit Sub
End Sub
```

STEP 3: Let us test it out!

Select any cell that you want to insert columns on. Go to **Developer > Code > Macros**

Make sure your Macro is selected. Click **Run**.

We want to insert 3 columns. **Type in 3**.

With that, you are now able to insert multiple columns using Macros!

	A	B	C	D	E	F
1	CUSTOMER	Column3	Column2	Column1	PRODUCTS	SALES PERSON
2	LONG ISLANDS INC				SOFT DRINKS	Michael Jackson
3	LONG ISLANDS INC				SOFT DRINKS	Michael Jackson
4	LONG ISLANDS INC				SOFT DRINKS	Michael Jackson
5	LONG ISLANDS INC				SOFT DRINKS	Michael Jackson
6	LONG ISLANDS INC				SOFT DRINKS	Michael Jackson
7	LONG ISLANDS INC				SOFT DRINKS	Michael Jackson
8	LONG ISLANDS INC				SOFT DRINKS	Michael Jackson
9	LONG ISLANDS INC				SOFT DRINKS	Michael Jackson
10	LONG ISLANDS INC				SOFT DRINKS	Michael Jackson

How to Insert Multiple Rows

What does it do?

Asks for a number of rows, then inserts it at the bottom of your selected cell

Copy Source Code:

```
Sub InsertMultipleRows()

Dim numRows As Integer
Dim counter As Integer

'Select the current row
ActiveCell.EntireRow.Select
On Error GoTo Last
numRows  = InputBox("Enter number of rows to insert", "Insert
Rows")

'Keep on inserting rows until we reach the desired number
For counter = 1 To numRows
Selection.Insert Shift:=xlToDown,
CopyOrigin:=xlFormatFromRightorAbove
Next counter
Last:Exit Sub
End Sub
```

Final Result:

	A	B	C	D
1	CUSTOMER	PRODUCTS	SALES PERSON	SALES REGION
2	LONG ISLANDS INC	SOFT DRINKS	Michael Jackson	AMERICAS
3				
4				
5				
6	LONG ISLANDS INC	SOFT DRINKS	Michael Jackson	AMERICAS
7	LONG ISLANDS INC	SOFT DRINKS	Michael Jackson	AMERICAS
8	LONG ISLANDS INC	SOFT DRINKS	Michael Jackson	AMERICAS
9	LONG ISLANDS INC	SOFT DRINKS	Michael Jackson	AMERICAS

Did you know you could **insert multiple rows using Macros in Excel?**

With just a loop and providing a number, you can do this in a single click!

STEP 1: Go to *Developer* > *Code* > *Visual Basic*

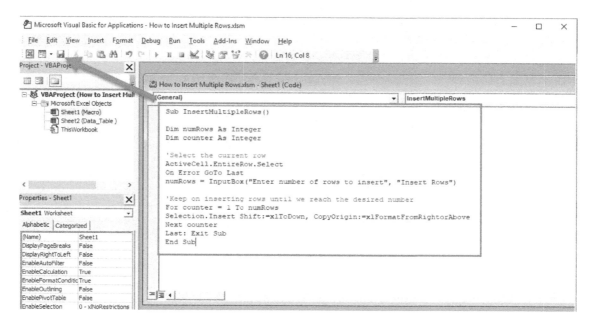

STEP 2: Make sure **Sheet1** is selected, paste in your code and **Select Save**. Close the window afterwards.

```vba
Sub InsertMultipleRows()

Dim numRows As Integer
Dim counter As Integer

'Select the current row
ActiveCell.EntireRow.Select
On Error GoTo Last
numRows = InputBox("Enter number of rows to insert", "Insert Rows")

'Keep on inserting rows until we reach the desired number
For counter = 1 To numRows
Selection.Insert Shift:=xlToDown, CopyOrigin:=xlFormatFromRightorAbove
Next counter
Last: Exit Sub
End Sub
```

STEP 3: Let us test it out!

Select any cell that you want to insert rows on. Go to *Developer* > *Code* > *Macros*

Make sure your Macro is selected. Click **Run**.

We want to insert 3 rows. **Type in 3**.

With that, you are now able to insert multiple rows using Macros!

	CUSTOMER	PRODUCTS	SALES PERSON	SALES REGION
1	CUSTOMER	PRODUCTS	SALES PERSON	SALES REGION
2	LONG ISLANDS INC	SOFT DRINKS	Michael Jackson	AMERICAS
3				
4				
5				
6	LONG ISLANDS INC	SOFT DRINKS	Michael Jackson	AMERICAS
7	LONG ISLANDS INC	SOFT DRINKS	Michael Jackson	AMERICAS
8	LONG ISLANDS INC	SOFT DRINKS	Michael Jackson	AMERICAS
9	LONG ISLANDS INC	SOFT DRINKS	Michael Jackson	AMERICAS

How to Insert Numbers

What does it do?

Asks for a max number, then generates numbers from 1 to the max number

Copy Source Code:

```
Sub InsertNumbers()

Dim maxNumber As Integer
Dim counter As Integer

On Error GoTo Last
maxNumber = InputBox("Enter the Max Value", "Generate 1 to n")
'Generate all the numbers
For counter = 1 To maxNumber
ActiveCell.Value = counter
'Move one cell below
ActiveCell.Offset(1, 0).Activate
Next counter
Last: Exit Sub
End Sub
```

Final Result:

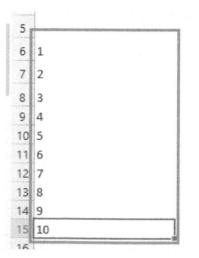

I wanted to insert consecutive numbers in a cool way. And the way I found was to **insert numbers using Macros in Excel!**

We get to learn to use a loop as well to do this!

STEP 1: Go to *Developer > Code > Visual Basic*

STEP 2: Make sure **Sheet1** is selected, paste in your code and **Select Save**. Close the window afterwards.

```
Sub InsertNumbers()

Dim maxNumber As Integer
Dim counter As Integer

On Error GoTo Last
maxNumber = InputBox("Enter the Max Value", "Generate 1 to n")
'Generate all the numbers
For counter = 1 To maxNumber
ActiveCell.Value = counter
'Move one cell below
ActiveCell.Offset(1, 0).Activate
Next counter
Last: Exit Sub
End Sub
```

STEP 3: Let us test it out!

Select any cell that you want to insert numbers on. Go to *Developer > Code > Macros*

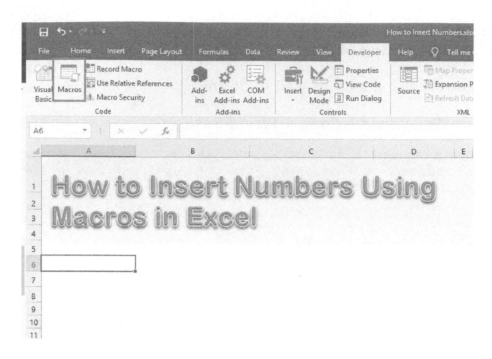

Make sure your Macro is selected. Click **Run**.

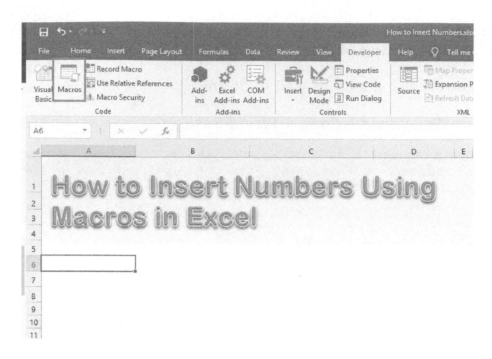

We want to insert 10 numbers. **Type in 10**.

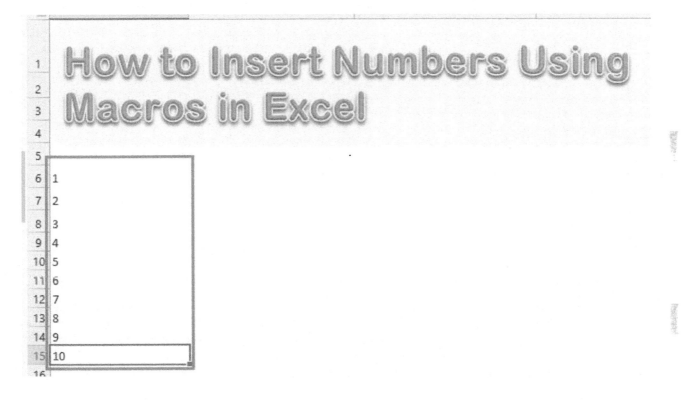

Generate 1 to n   ✕

Enter the Max Value   OK

Cancel

10

With that, you are now able to insert consecutive numbers using Macros!

How to Remove Text Wrap

What does it do?

Removes text wrap in all cells and then autofit all of the cells

Copy Source Code:

```
Sub RemoveWrapAndAutofitCells()
Activate
Cells.Select

'Remove the Text Wrap
Selection.WrapText = False

'Autofit all of the cells afterwards
Cells.EntireRow.AutoFit
Cells.EntireColumn.AutoFit
End Sub
```

Final Result:

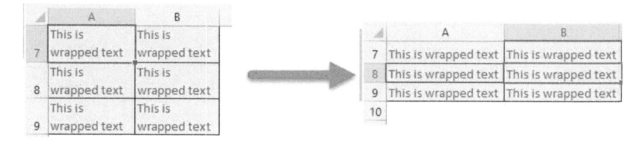

Ever wanted to remove all the text wrapping, but the hassle of your cells spilling over is stopping you? Have no fear, Macros are here to save the day! You can **remove text wrap using Macros in Excel** then autofit the cells as well!

STEP 1: Go to *Developer > Code > Visual Basic*

STEP 2: Paste in your code and **Select Save**. Close the window afterwards.

```
Sub RemoveWrapAndAutofitCells()
Activate
Cells.Select

'Remove the Text Wrap
Selection.WrapText = False

'Autofit all of the cells afterwards
Cells.EntireRow.AutoFit
Cells.EntireColumn.AutoFit
End Sub
```

STEP 3: Let us test it out!

Open the sheet containing the data. Go to ***Developer > Code > Macros***

Make sure your Macro is selected. Click **Run**.

Macro		? ✕
Macro name:		
Sheet1.RemoveWrapAndAutofitCells	⬆	Run
Sheet1.RemoveWrapAndAutofitCells		Step Into
		Edit
		Create
		Delete
		Options...
Macros in:	All Open Workbooks	
Description		
		Cancel

With just one click, all of the cells now have text wrap removed!

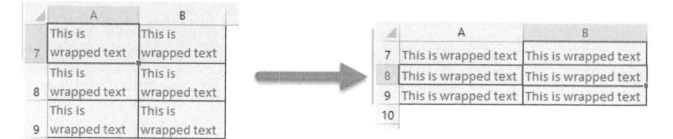

Unmerge Cells

What does it do?

Unmerge the selection of cells

Copy Source Code:

```
Sub UnmergeAllCells()
'Unmerge all cells in one go!
Selection.UnMerge
End Sub
```

Final Result:

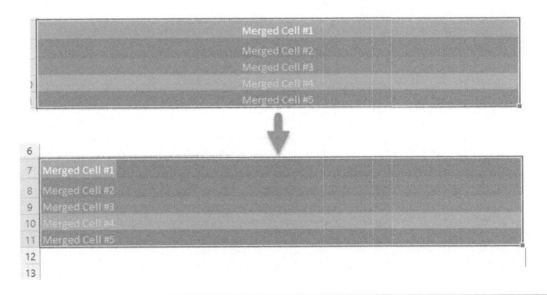

Excel provides us a way to **unmerge all cells** through its interface. Did you know that you can do the same thing with Excel Macros? Let us try out this exercise!

STEP 1: Go to *Developer > Code > Visual Basic*

STEP 2: Paste in your code and **Select Save**. Close the window afterwards.

```vba
Sub UnmergeAllCells()

'Unmerge all cells in one go!
Selection.UnMerge

End Sub
```

STEP 3: Let us test it out!

Make sure you have selected your merged cells for unmerging. Go to ***Developer > Code > Macros***

Make sure your Macro is selected. Click **Run**.

With just one click, **all of the cells are now unmerged**!

Use Calculator

What does it do?

Launch the Calculator from Excel

Copy Source Code:

```
Sub UseCalculator()

'Open the Calculator for quick calculations
Application.ActivateMicrosoftApp Index:=0

End Sub
```

Final Result:

Inside Excel, there is that cool functionality of launching the **calculator** from there, and you can do that with Excel Macros! You can now perform some quick calculations using the calculator.

STEP 1: Go to *Developer > Code > Visual Basic*

STEP 2: Paste in your code and **Select Save**. Close the window afterwards.

STEP 3: Let us test it out!

Go to *Developer > Code > Macros*

Make sure your Macro is selected. Click **Run.**

With just one click, **you have launched the calculator inside Excel**!

CHART MACROS

Add Chart Title

What does it do?

Adds a title to the selected chart based on user input

Copy Source Code:

```vba
'Make sure you have selected your chart first
Sub AddChartTitle()

Dim titleText As Variant

On Error GoTo Last
'Get the Chart Title from the user
titleText = InputBox("Please enter the chart title", "Chart
Title Input")

'Now set the title on the selected chart
ActiveChart.SetElement (msoElementChartTitleAboveChart)
ActiveChart.ChartTitle.Text = titleText
Last: Exit Sub

End Sub
```

Final Result:

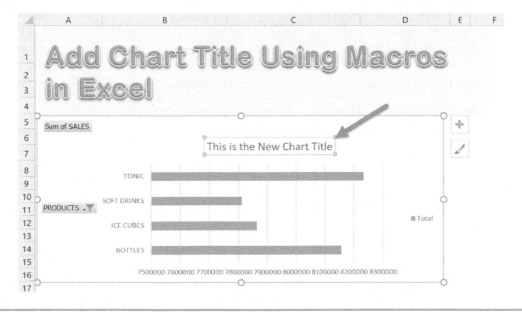

Did you know that you can programmatically make changes to Excel Charts?
Yes you can! Let us try updating a chart by **adding the chart title** using Excel
Macros!

This is our starting chart:

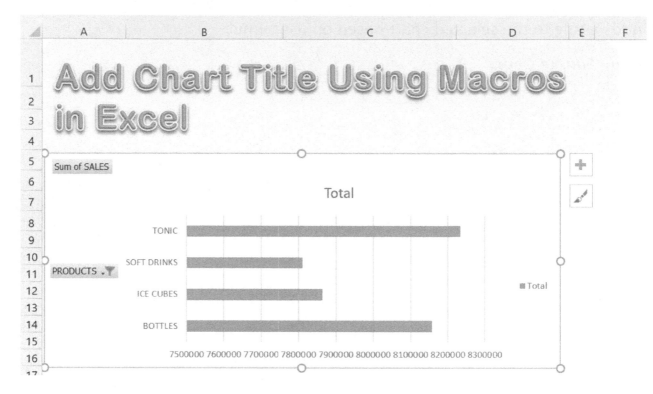

STEP 1: Go to *Developer > Code > Visual Basic*

STEP 2: Paste in your code and **Select Save**. Close the window afterwards.

```
'Make sure you have selected your chart first
Sub AddChartTitle()

Dim titleText As Variant

On Error GoTo Last
'Get the Chart Title from the user
titleText = InputBox("Please enter the chart title", "Chart Title Input")

'Now set the title on the selected chart
ActiveChart.SetElement (msoElementChartTitleAboveChart)
ActiveChart.ChartTitle.Text = titleText
Last: Exit Sub

End Sub
```

STEP 3: Let us test it out!

Open the sheet containing the chart. Make sure your chart is selected. Go to **Developer > Code > Macros**

Make sure your Macro is selected. Click **Run**.

Type in the title you want for your chart. **Click OK.**

Chart Title Input   ✕

Please enter the chart title   ┌──────────┐
                                                          │   OK   │
                                                          └──────────┘

                                                             Cancel

This is the New Chart Title

With just that, **you have modified the chart title**!

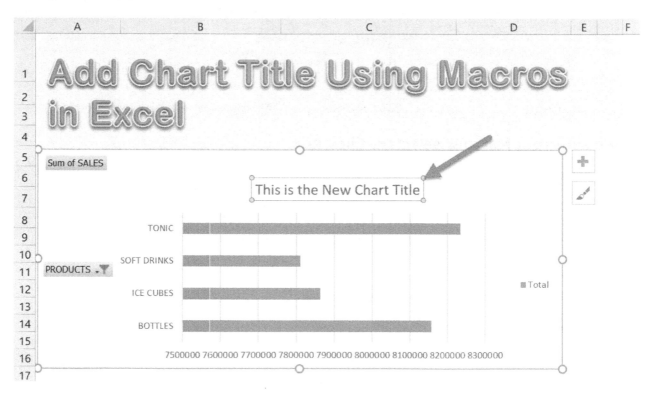

Change Chart Type

What does it do?

Change the chart type to your specified type

Copy Source Code:

```
'Select your chart first before running this
Sub ChangeChartType()

'This is the clustered column chart, you can change the type
'Other chart types are listed at: https://docs.microsoft.com/en-us/office/vba/api/Excel.XlChartType
ActiveChart.ChartType = xlColumnClustered

End Sub
```

Final Result:

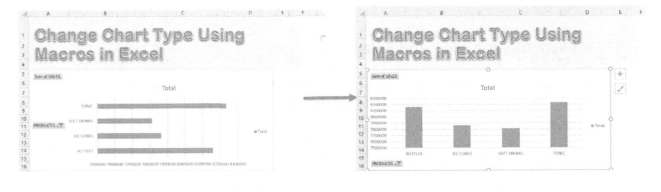

Macros encompass a lot of functionalities, and one of them is changing the properties of Charts! Let us try to **change the chart type** using Excel Macros!

This is our original bar chart. Let us change it to a **Clustered Column Chart**:

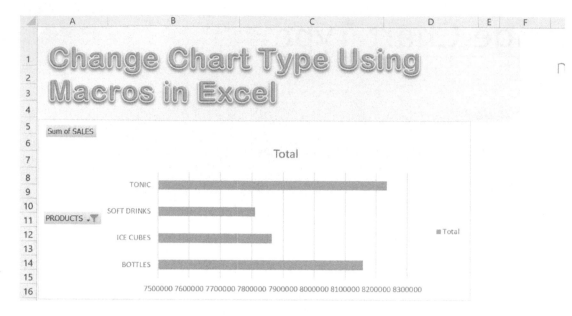

STEP 1: Go to *Developer* > *Code* > *Visual Basic*

STEP 2: Paste in your code and **Select Save**.

You can change the chart type in the code to the type you prefer. The list of chart types are listed here: https://docs.microsoft.com/en-us/office/vba/api/Excel.XlChartType

Close the window afterwards.

```vba
'Select your chart first before running this
Sub ChangeChartType()

'This is the clustered column chart, you can change the type
'Other chart types are listed at: https://docs.microsoft.com/en-us/office/vba/api/Excel.XlChartType
ActiveChart.ChartType = xlColumnClustered

End Sub
```

STEP 3: Let us test it out!

Open the sheet containing the chart. Make sure your chart is selected. Go to *Developer > Code > Macros*

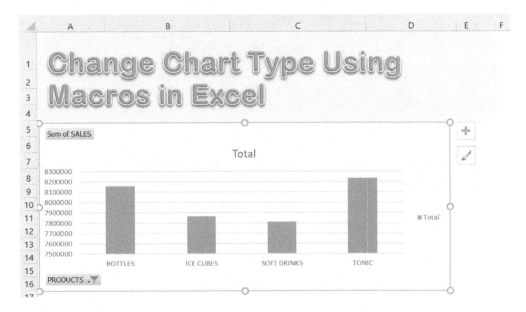

Make sure your Macro is selected. Click **Run**.

With just one click, **your chart type is now changed**!

Convert Chart into Image

What does it do?

Converts your selected chart into an image

Copy Source Code:

```
'Make sure you have selected your chart first
Sub ConvertChartIntoImage()

ActiveChart.ChartArea.Copy
ActiveSheet.Range("A1").Select
'Converts the Chart into an Image
'Then it gets pasted on Cell A1 of the active sheet
ActiveSheet.Pictures.Paste.Select
End Sub
```

Final Result:

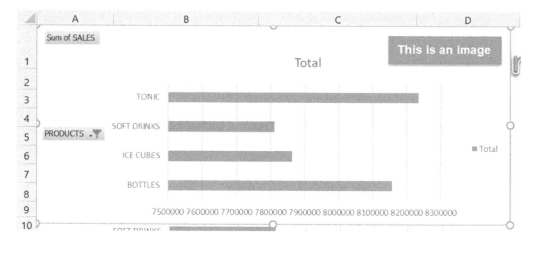

Wanted to save your chart as in image to use elsewhere? You can use Excel Macros to **convert your selected chart into an image**!

This is our chart that we want to convert:

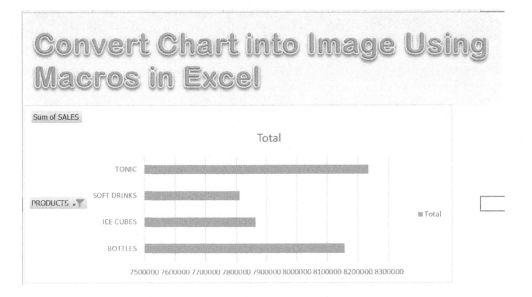

STEP 1: Go to ***Developer > Code > Visual Basic***

STEP 2: Paste in your code and **Select Save**. Close the window afterwards.

```
'Make sure you have selected your chart first
Sub ConvertChartIntoImage()

ActiveChart.ChartArea.Copy
ActiveSheet.Range("A1").Select

'Converts the Chart into an Image
'Then it gets pasted on Cell A1 of the active sheet
ActiveSheet.Pictures.Paste.Select

End Sub
```

STEP 3: Let us test it out!

Open the sheet containing the chart. Make sure your chart is selected. Go to ***Developer > Code > Macros***

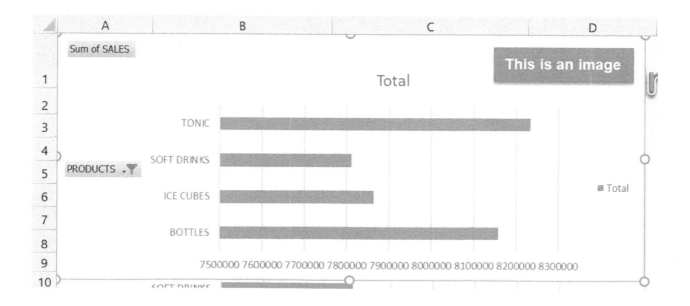

Make sure your Macro is selected. Click **Run**.

With just one click, **your chart is now converted into an image**!

Resize All Charts

What does it do?

Resizes all charts to a specific height and width

Copy Source Code:

```
'Make sure to change the Width and Height values below
Sub ResizeAllCharts()

Dim counter As Integer

'Loop through all of the charts
For counter = 1 To ActiveSheet.ChartObjects.Count
'Change the Height and Width values based on your requirements
With ActiveSheet.ChartObjects(counter)
.Height = 400
.Width = 400
End With
Next counter

End Sub
```

Final Result:

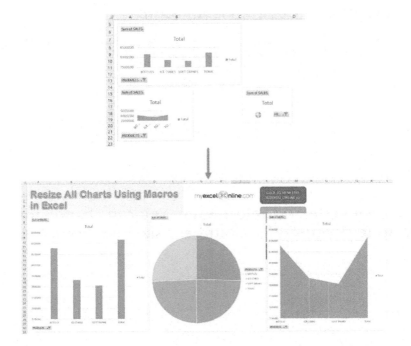

Have a lot of charts and want to keep them organized to a consistent size?
Excel Macros can **resize all charts** with a single click!

These are our charts:

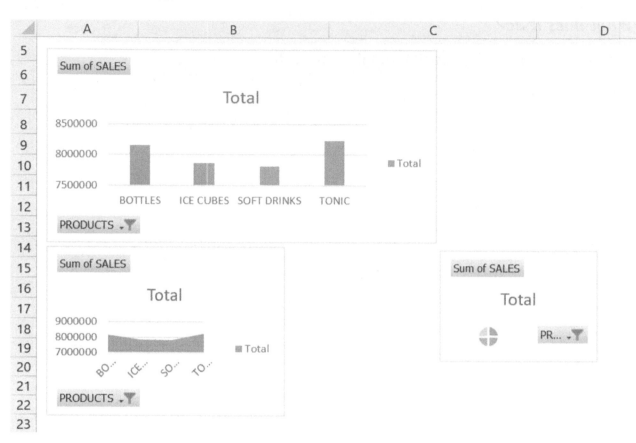

STEP 1: Go to *Developer > Code > Visual Basic*

STEP 2: Paste in your code and **Select Save**. You can change the
Height and **Weight** if you prefer a different size than 400. Close the window
afterwards.

Microsoft Visual Basic for Applications - Resize All Charts.xlsm - [Sheet1 (Code)]

```vba
'Make sure to change the Width and Height values below
Sub ResizeAllCharts()

Dim counter As Integer

'Loop through all of the charts
For counter = 1 To ActiveSheet.ChartObjects.Count
'Change the Height and Width values based on your requirements
With ActiveSheet.ChartObjects(counter)
.Height = 400
.Width = 400
End With
Next counter

End Sub
```

STEP 3: Let us test it out!

Open the sheet containing the charts. Go to *Developer > Code > Macros*

Make sure your Macro is selected. Click **Run**.

With just one click, **all of your charts are now resized**!

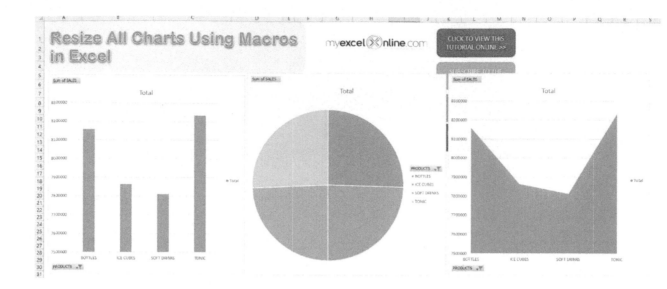

FORMULA MACROS

Add a Degree Symbol to Selection

What does it do?

Adds a degree symbol to each number in your selection

Copy Source Code:

```
Sub AddDegreeSymbolToSelection()
Dim rng As Range
'Loop through the entire selection
For Each rng In Selection
'Set the active cell
rng.Select
'For each number, add the degree symbol at the end
If ActiveCell <> "" Then
If IsNumeric(ActiveCell.Value) Then
ActiveCell.Value = ActiveCell.Value & "°"
End If
End If
Next
End Sub
```

Final Result:

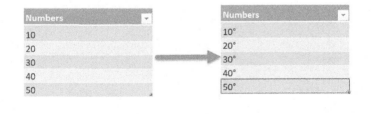

Have numbers that are degrees but you are having difficulty inserting the degree symbol to each? Excel Macros can modify your numbers and you will **add a degree symbol** to your selection in a single click!

You will learn here on how you can customize text and modify it using Macros.

This is our list of numbers:

Numbers
10
20
30
40
50

STEP 1: Go to *Developer > Code > Visual Basic*

STEP 2: Paste in your code and **Select Save**. Close the window afterwards.

```
Sub AddDegreeSymbolToSelection()

Dim rng As range

'Loop through the entire selection
For Each rng In Selection
'Set the active cell
rng.Select
'For each number, add the degree symbol at the end
If ActiveCell <> "" Then
If IsNumeric(ActiveCell.Value) Then
ActiveCell.Value = ActiveCell.Value & "°"
End If
End If
Next

End Sub
```

STEP 3: Let us test it out!

Open the sheet containing the data. Make sure your data is highlighted. Go to *Developer > Code > Macros*

Make sure your Macro is selected. Click **Run**.

With just one click, **all your numbers have the degree symbol added to it**!

Add letters A-Z

What does it do?

Adds the letters A to Z

Copy Source Code:

```
Sub AddLettersAtoZ()
Dim counter As Integer
'Let us use the ascii codes of the alphabet - A(65) to Z(90)
For counter = 65 To 90
ActiveCell.Value= Chr(counter)
'Move to one cell down
ActiveCell.Offset(1, 0).Select
Next counter
End Sub
```

Final Result:

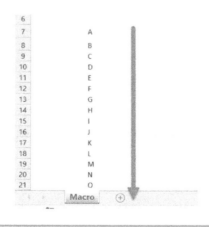

Excel Macros is very powerful and allows you to do a lot of fun things. Let us try to use loops and **add letters A-Z** with just a single click!

STEP 1: Go to *Developer > Code > Visual Basic*

STEP 2: Paste in your code and **Select Save**. Close the window afterwards.

```
Sub AddLettersAtoZ()

Dim counter As Integer

'Let us use the ascii codes of the alphabet - A(65) to Z(90)
For counter = 65 To 90
ActiveCell.Value = Chr(counter)
'Move to one cell down
ActiveCell.Offset(1, 0).Select
Next counter

End Sub
```

STEP 3: Let us test it out!

Go to *Developer > Code > Macros*

Make sure your Macro is selected. Click **Run**.

With just one click, **all of the letters A-Z are added in a single click**!

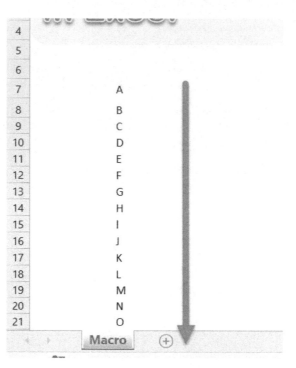

	A	B
13		G
14		H
15		I
16		J
17		K
18		L
19		M
20		N
21		O
22		P
23		Q
24		R
25		S
26		T
27		U
28		V
29		W
30		X
31		Y
32		Z

Calculate Square Root

What does it do?

Calculate the square root of your selected numbers

Copy Source Code:

```
'Make sure you have a range of numbers selected
Sub CalculateSquareRoot()
Dim rng As Range
'Loop through all of the cells
For Each rng In Selection
'If it is a number, then get the square root
If WorksheetFunction.IsNumber(rng) Then
rng.Value= Sqr(rng)
Else
End If
Next rng
End Sub
```

Final Result:

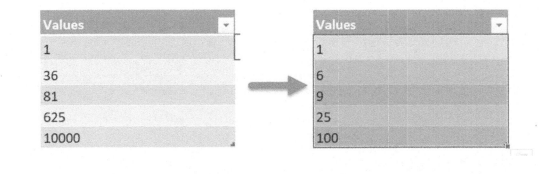

Excel Macros are capable of doing a lot of things, and mathematical calculations is one of them! Let us use Excel Macros to **calculate the square root of your selected numbers**!

Here are the numbers that we want to get the square root of:

Values
1
36
81
625
10000

STEP 1: Go to *Developer > Code > Visual Basic*

STEP 2: Paste in your code and **Select Save**. Close the window afterwards.

```vba
'Make sure you have a range of numbers selected
Sub CalculateSquareRoot()

Dim rng As range

'Loop through all of the cells
For Each rng In Selection
'If it is a number, then get the square root
If WorksheetFunction.IsNumber(rng) Then
rng.Value = Sqr(rng)
Else
End If
Next rng

End Sub
```

STEP 3: Let us test it out!

Open the sheet containing the data. Make sure your numbers are highlighted.
Go to *Developer > Code > Macros*

Make sure your Macro is selected. Click **Run**.

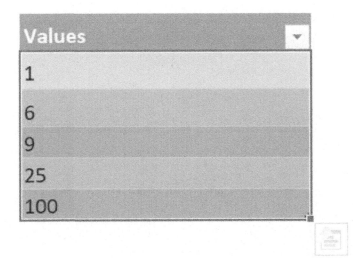

With just one click, **you have calculated the square root of all your numbers**!

Values
1
6
9
25
100

Convert Date into Day

What does it do?

Convert your selected date into day values

Copy Source Code:

```
'Make sure you have selected a range of cells first
Sub ConvertDateIntoDay()

Dim cell As Range
Selection.Value = Selection.Value

'Check each cell
For Each cell In Selection
'If it is a date, then extract the day from it
If IsDate(cell) = True Then
With cell
.Value = Day(cell)
.NumberFormat = "0"
End With
End If
Next cell

End Sub
```

Final Result:

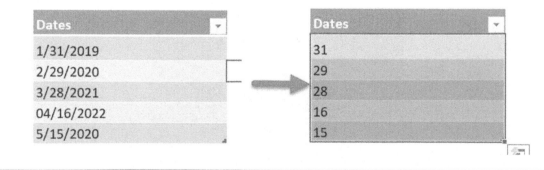

Macros are also capable of processing dates and times. Let us see how we can **convert date into day values** using Excel Macros!

These are our dates to convert:

Dates	
1/31/2019	
2/29/2020	
3/28/2021	
04/16/2022	
5/15/2020	

STEP 1: Go to *Developer > Code > Visual Basic*

STEP 2: Paste in your code and **Select Save**. Close the window afterwards.

STEP 3: Let us test it out!

Open the sheet containing the data. Make sure your data is highlighted. Go to *Developer > Code > Macros*

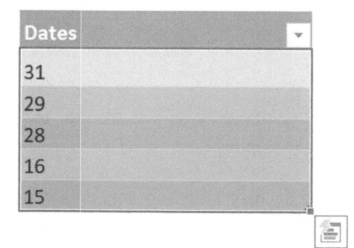

| File | Home | Insert | Page Layout | Formulas | Data | Review | View | Developer | Help | Power Pivot | ⚲ Tell me what y |

Visual Basic | Macros | Use Relative References / Macro Security — Code | Add-ins | Excel Add-ins | COM Add-ins — Add-ins | Insert ▾ | Design Mode — Controls | Properties / View Code / Run Dialog | Source | Map Properties / Expansion Packs / Refresh Data — XML | Import / Export

Make sure your Macro is selected. Click **Run**.

Macro		? ✕
Macro name:		
Sheet1.ConvertDateIntoDay	⬆	Run
Sheet1.ConvertDateIntoDay	⌃	Step Into
		Edit
		Create
		Delete
	⌄	Options...
Macros in:	All Open Workbooks ⌄	
Description		

Dates
1/31/2019
2/29/2020
3/28/2021
04/16/2022
5/15/2020

With just one click, **all of your dates are now converted to days**!

Dates
31
29
28
16
15

Convert Date into Month

What does it do?

Convert your selected date into month values

Copy Source Code:

```
'Make sure you have selected a range of cells first
Sub ConvertDateIntoMonth()

Dim cell As Range
Selection.Value = Selection.Value

'Check each cell
For Each cell In Selection
'If it is a date, then extract the month from it
If IsDate(cell) = True Then
With cell
.Value = Month(cell)
.NumberFormat = "0"
End With
End If
Next cell

End Sub
```

Final Result:

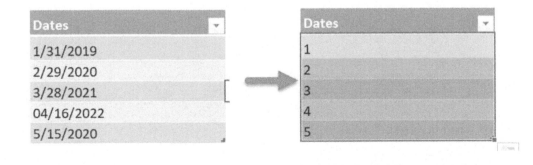

Macros are also capable of processing dates and times. Let us see how we can **convert date into month values** using Excel Macros!

These are our dates to convert:

Dates	
1/31/2019	
2/29/2020	
3/28/2021	
04/16/2022	
5/15/2020	

STEP 1: Go to *Developer > Code > Visual Basic*

STEP 2: Paste in your code and **Select Save**. Close the window afterwards.

```vba
'Make sure you have selected a range of cells first
Sub ConvertDateIntoMonth()

Dim cell As Range
Selection.Value = Selection.Value

'Check each cell
For Each cell In Selection
'If it is a date, then extract the month from it
If IsDate(cell) = True Then
With cell
.Value = Month(cell)
.NumberFormat = "0"
End With
End If
Next cell

End Sub
```

STEP 3: Let us test it out!

Open the sheet containing the data. Make sure your data is highlighted. Go to *Developer > Code > Macros*

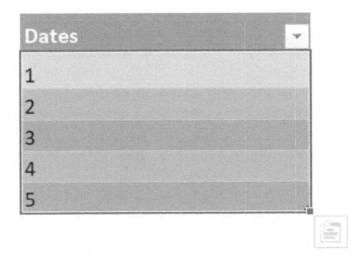

Make sure your Macro is selected. Click **Run**.

With just one click, **all of your dates are now converted to months**!

Convert Date into Year

What does it do?

Convert your selected date into year values

Copy Source Code:

```vba
'Make sure you have selected a range of cells first
Sub ConvertDateIntoYear()

Dim cell As Range
Selection.Value = Selection.Value

'Check each cell
For Each cell In Selection
'If it is a date, then extract the year from it
If IsDate(cell) = True Then
With cell
.Value = Year(cell)
.NumberFormat = "0"
End With
End If
Next cell

End Sub
```

Final Result:

Dates	▼
1/31/2019	
2/29/2020	
3/28/2021	
04/16/2022	
5/15/2020	

→

Dates	▼
2019	
2020	
2021	
2022	
2020	

Macros are also capable of processing dates and times. Let us see how we can **convert date into year values** using Excel Macros!

These are our dates to convert:

Dates	
1/31/2019	
2/29/2020	
3/28/2021	
04/16/2022	
5/15/2020	

STEP 1: Go to *Developer > Code > Visual Basic*

STEP 2: Paste in your code and **Select Save**. Close the window afterwards.

```vba
'Make sure you have selected a range of cells first
Sub ConvertDateIntoYear()

Dim cell As Range
Selection.Value = Selection.Value

'Check each cell
For Each cell In Selection
'If it is a date, then extract the year from it
If IsDate(cell) = True Then
With cell
.Value = Year(cell)
.NumberFormat = "0"
End With
End If
Next cell

End Sub
```

STEP 3: Let us test it out!

Open the sheet containing the data. Make sure your data is highlighted. Go to *Developer > Code > Macros*

Make sure your Macro is selected. Click **Run**.

With just one click, **all of your dates are now converted to years**!

Convert Formulas into Values

What does it do?

Converts formulas into values in your selection

Copy Source Code:

```
Sub ConvertFormulasIntoValues()

Dim rng As Range
Dim formulaCell As Range
Set rng = Selection

'Check each cell in the range if it has a formula
For Each formulaCell In rng
If formulaCell.HasFormula Then
formulaCell.Formula = formulaCell.Value
End If
Next formulaCell

End Sub
```

Final Result:

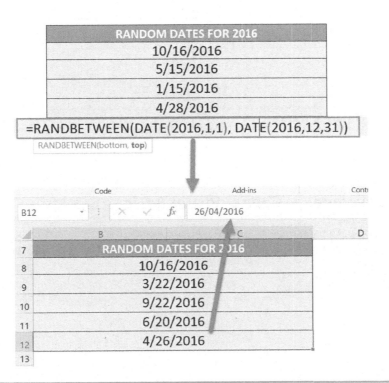

Whenever we have a lot of cells with formulas, then want to change them to permanent values, we need to use the Paste Special. What if I told you, you can do this in a single click for all formula cells in your selection?

That's right, Excel Macros can **convert formulas into values** in one step!

Here is our list of formula cells:

RANDOM DATES FOR 2016
10/16/2016
5/15/2016
1/15/2016
4/28/2016
8/1/2016

To have a better look, you can see it uses the **RANDBETWEEN** formula. Let us change these to values only!

RANDOM DATES FOR 2016
10/16/2016
5/15/2016
1/15/2016
4/28/2016

=RANDBETWEEN(DATE(2016,1,1), DATE(2016,12,31))

RANDBETWEEN(bottom, **top**)

STEP 1: Go to *Developer > Code > Visual Basic*

STEP 2: Paste in your code and **Select Save**. Close the window afterwards.

STEP 3: Let us test it out!

Open the sheet containing the data. Make sure your formula cells are highlighted. Go to **Developer > Code > Macros**

Make sure your Macro is selected. Click **Run**.

With just one click, **all of the formula cells are now converted to values**! The values also changed because of the nature of the RANDBETWEEN formula, as it changes along with any change done to the workbook.

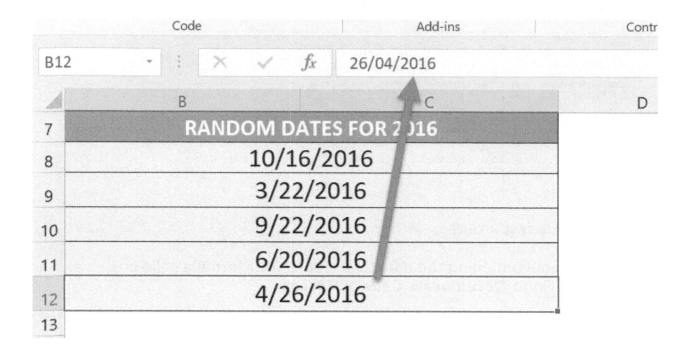

Convert Negative Numbers to Positive

What does it do?

Converts your selected numbers to positive

Copy Source Code:

```
'Make sure you have a selection of negative numbers ready
Sub ConvertNegativeNumbersToPositive()

Dim rng As range

Selection.Value = Selection.Value

'Loop through the cells
For Each rng In Selection
'If it is a number, then convert it into a positive value
If WorksheetFunction.IsNumber(rng) Then rng.Value = Abs(rng)
Next rng

End Sub
```

Final Result:

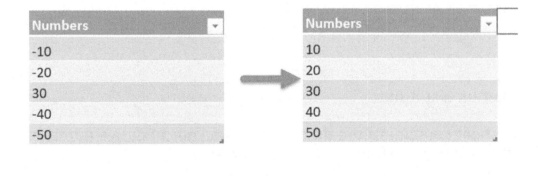

Have a range of numbers where you want to convert them to all positive? We can use Excel Macros to **convert negative numbers to positive** with one click!

These are our selection of negative numbers:

Numbers
-10
-20
30
-40
-50

STEP 1: Go to *Developer > Code > Visual Basic*

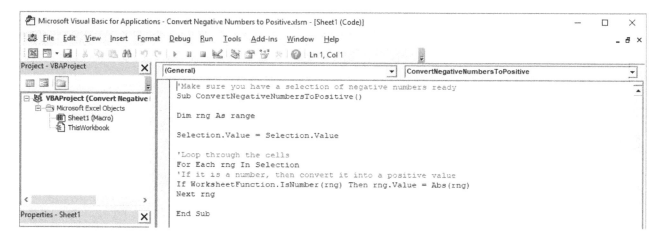

STEP 2: Paste in your code and **Select Save**. Close the window afterwards.

```
'Make sure you have a selection of negative numbers ready
Sub ConvertNegativeNumbersToPositive()

Dim rng As range

Selection.Value = Selection.Value

'Loop through the cells
For Each rng In Selection
'If it is a number, then convert it into a positive value
If WorksheetFunction.IsNumber(rng) Then rng.Value = Abs(rng)
Next rng

End Sub
```

STEP 3: Let us test it out!

Open the sheet containing the data. Make sure your negative numbers are highlighted. Go to *Developer > Code > Macros*

Make sure your Macro is selected. Click **Run**.

With just one click, **all of your numbers are now converted to positive**!

Convert Roman Numbers into Modern Numbers

What does it do?

Converts your selected Roman Numbers Into Arabic

Copy Source Code:

```vba
'Make sure you have a selection of roman numbers ready
Sub ConvertRomanNumbersIntoArabic()

Dim rng As Range

Selection.Value = Selection.Value

'Loop through all of the cells
For Each rng In Selection
If Not WorksheetFunction.IsNonText(rng) Then
'This is where the magic happens, it converts it to arabic
numbers
rng.Value= WorksheetFunction.Arabic(rng)
End If
Next rng

End Sub
```

Final Result:

Roman Numbers ▼
XXVII
XXXII
DLV
MDLXXXIV
CLXXXIII

Roman Numbers ▼
27
32
555
1584
183

Ever seen Roman Numbers that you want to simply convert to normal numbers? Excel Macros can do the hard work for you and convert **Roman Numbers into Arabic** with one click!

These are the Roman Numbers that we want to convert to Arabic:

Roman Numbers	▼
XXVII	
XXXII	
DLV	
MDLXXXIV	
CLXXXIII	

STEP 1: Go to *Developer* > *Code* > *Visual Basic*

STEP 2: Paste in your code and **Select Save**. Close the window afterwards.

```vba
'Make sure you have a selection of roman numbers ready
Sub ConvertRomanNumbersIntoArabic()

Dim rng As range

Selection.Value = Selection.Value

'Loop through all of the cells
For Each rng In Selection
If Not WorksheetFunction.IsNonText(rng) Then
'This is where the magic happens, it converts it to arabic numbers
rng.Value = WorksheetFunction.Arabic(rng)
End If
Next rng

End Sub
```

STEP 3: Let us test it out!

Open the sheet containing the data. Make sure your Roman Numbers are highlighted. Go to *Developer > Code > Macros*

Make sure your Macro is selected. Click **Run**.

With just one click, **all of the Roman Numbers are now converted correctly**!

Roman Numbers
27
32
555
1584
183

Convert Selection to Lower Case

What does it do?

Converts selected text to lower case

Copy Source Code:

```
'Make sure you have selected a range first
Sub ConvertSelectionToLowerCase()
Dim rng As Range
For Each rng In Selection
'Check if this is text first, then convert into lower case
If Application.WorksheetFunction.IsText(rng) Then
rng.Value = LCase(rng)
End If
Next
End Sub
```

Final Result:

When it comes to cleaning up text, Excel Macros can make short work of it. You can create Macros to **convert selection to lower case** with one click!

This is our text. Let us do some clean up!

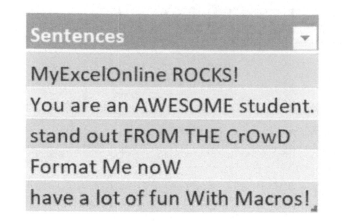

STEP 1: Go to *Developer > Code > Visual Basic*

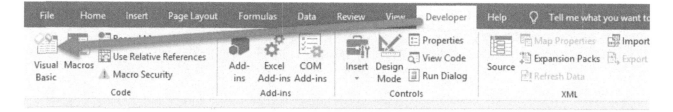

STEP 2: Paste in your code and **Select Save**. Close the window afterwards.

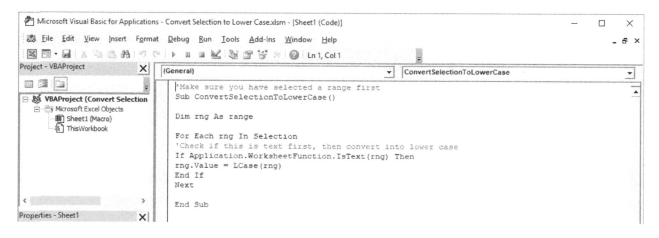

STEP 3: Let us test it out!

Open the sheet containing the data. Make sure your data is highlighted. Go to *Developer > Code > Macros*

Make sure your Macro is selected. Click **Run**.

With just one click, **all of the cells now converted to lower case**!

Convert Selection to Proper Case

What does it do?

Converts selected text to proper case

Copy Source Code:

```
'Make sure you have selected a range first
Sub ConvertSelectionToProperCase()
Dim rng As Range
For Each rng In Selection
'Check if this is text first, then convert into proper case
If Application.WorksheetFunction.IsText(rng) Then
rng.Value = Application.WorksheetFunction.Proper(rng)
End If
Next
End Sub
```

Final Result:

Sentences ▾
MyExcelOnline ROCKS!
You are an AWESOME student.
stand out FROM THE CrOwD
Format Me noW
have a lot of fun With Macros!

➡

Sentences ▾
Myexcelonline Rocks!
You Are An Awesome Student.
Stand Out From The Crowd
Format Me Now
Have A Lot Of Fun With Macros!

When it comes to cleaning up text, Excel Macros can make short work of it. You can create Macros to **convert selection to proper case** with one click!

This is our text. Let us do some clean up!

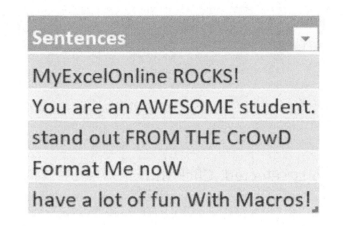

STEP 1: Go to *Developer > Code > Visual Basic*

STEP 2: Paste in your code and **Select Save**. Close the window afterwards.

```vba
'Make sure you have selected a range first
Sub ConvertSelectionToProperCase()

Dim rng As range

For Each rng In Selection
'Check if this is text first, then convert into proper case
If Application.WorksheetFunction.IsText(rng) Then
rng.Value = Application.WorksheetFunction.Proper(rng)
End If
Next

End Sub
```

STEP 3: Let us test it out!

Open the sheet containing the data. Make sure your data is highlighted. Go to *Developer > Code > Macros*

File	Home	Insert	Page Layout	Formulas	Data	Review	View	Developer	Help	Power Pivot	♀ Tell me what yo

Visual Basic | Macros | Use Relative References | Macro Security | Add-ins | Excel Add-ins | COM Add-ins | Insert | Design Mode | Properties | View Code | Run Dialog | Source | Map Properties | Expansion Packs | Refresh Data | Import | Export

Code | Add-ins | Controls | XML

Make sure your Macro is selected. Click **Run**.

Macro ? ✕

Macro name:

Sheet1.ConvertSelectionToProperCase ⬆

Sheet1.ConvertSelectionToProperCase

Run

Step Into

Edit

Create

Delete

Options...

Macros in: All Open Workbooks

Description

Cancel

Sentences

MyExcelOnline ROCKS!
You are an AWESOME student.
stand out FROM THE CrOwD
Format Me noW
have a lot of fun With Macros!

With just one click, **all of the cells now converted to proper case**!

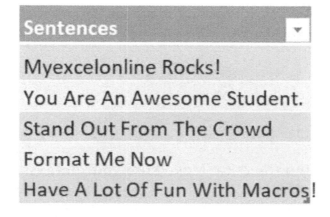

Sentences

Myexcelonline Rocks!
You Are An Awesome Student.
Stand Out From The Crowd
Format Me Now
Have A Lot Of Fun With Macros!

Convert Selection to Sentence Case

What does it do?

Converts selected text to sentence case

Copy Source Code:

```
'Make sure you have selected a range first
'Assumption is each cell is a single sentence
Sub ConvertSelectionToSentenceCase()

Dim rng As Range

For Each rng In Selection
'Check if this is text first, then convert into sentence case
'Make the first letter capitalized, then the rest of the text as
small letters
If Application.WorksheetFunction.IsText(rng) Then
rng.Value= UCase(Left(rng, 1)) & LCase(Right(rng, Len(rng) -1))
End If
Next

End Sub
```

Final Result:

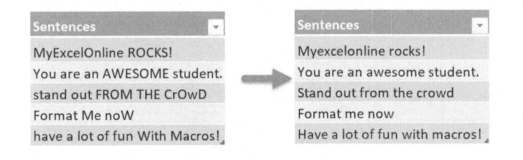

When it comes to cleaning up text, Excel Macros can make short work of it. You can create Macros to **convert selection to sentence case** with one click!

This is our text. Let us do some clean up!

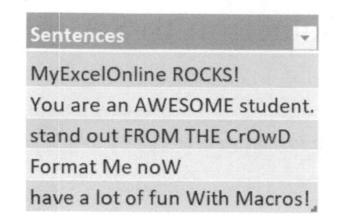

STEP 1: Go to *Developer > Code > Visual Basic*

STEP 2: Paste in your code and **Select Save**. Close the window afterwards.

```
'Make sure you have selected a range first
'Assumption is each cell is a single sentence
Sub ConvertSelectionToSentenceCase()

Dim rng As range

For Each rng In Selection
'Check if this is text first, then convert into sentence case
'Make the first letter capitalized, then the rest of the text as small letters
If Application.WorksheetFunction.IsText(rng) Then
rng.Value = UCase(Left(rng, 1)) & LCase(Right(rng, Len(rng) - 1))
End If
Next

End Sub
```

STEP 3: Let us test it out!

Open the sheet containing the data. Make sure your data is highlighted. Go to *Developer > Code > Macros*

Make sure your Macro is selected. Click **Run**.

With just one click, **all of the cells now converted to sentence case**!

Convert Selection to Upper Case

What does it do?

Converts selected text to upper case

Copy Source Code:

```vba
'Make sure you have selected a range first
Sub ConvertSelectionToUpperCase()
Dim rng As Range
For Each rng In Selection
'Check if this is text first, then convert into upper case
If Application.WorksheetFunction.IsText(rng) Then
rng.Value = UCase(rng)
End If
Next
End Sub
```

Final Result:

Sentences ▼
MyExcelOnline ROCKS!
You are an AWESOME student.
stand out FROM THE CrOwD
Format Me noW
have a lot of fun With Macros!

→

Sentences ▼
MYEXCELONLINE ROCKS!
YOU ARE AN AWESOME STUDENT.
STAND OUT FROM THE CROWD
FORMAT ME NOW
HAVE A LOT OF FUN WITH MACROS!

When it comes to cleaning up text, Excel Macros can make short work of it. You can create Macros to **convert selection to upper case** with one click!

This is our text. Let us do some clean up!

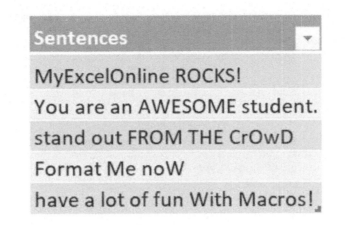

Sentences	▼
MyExcelOnline ROCKS!	
You are an AWESOME student.	
stand out FROM THE CrOwD	
Format Me noW	
have a lot of fun With Macros!	

STEP 1: Go to *Developer > Code > Visual Basic*

STEP 2: Paste in your code and **Select Save**. Close the window afterwards.

```
'Make sure you have selected a range first
Sub ConvertSelectionToUpperCase()

Dim rng As range

For Each rng In Selection
'Check if this is text first, then convert into upper case
If Application.WorksheetFunction.IsText(rng) Then
rng.Value = UCase(rng)
End If
Next

End Sub
```

STEP 3: Let us test it out!

Open the sheet containing the data. Make sure your data is highlighted. Go to *Developer > Code > Macros*

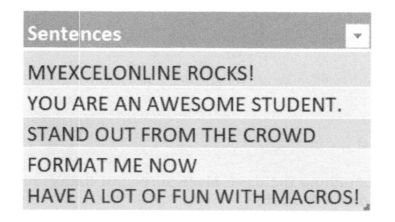

Make sure your Macro is selected. Click **Run**.

With just one click, **all of the cells now converted to upper case**!

Convert Time into Hour

What does it do?

Convert your selected time into hour values

Copy Source Code:

```
'Make sure you have selected a range of cells first
Sub ConvertTimeIntoHour()
Dim cell As Range
Selection.Value = Selection.Value
'Check each cell
For Each cell In Selection
'Extract the hour from it
With cell
.Value = Hour(cell)
.NumberFormat = "0"
End With
Next cell
End Sub
```

Final Result:

Macros are also capable of processing dates and times. Let us see how we can **convert time into hour values** using Excel Macros!

These are our times to convert:

Times
5:00:05 PM
1:23:45 AM
14:30:00
23:55
12:55:32 PM

STEP 1: Go to *Developer > Code > Visual Basic*

STEP 2: Paste in your code and **Select Save**. Close the window afterwards.

```
'Make sure you have selected a range of cells first
Sub ConvertTimeIntoHour()

Dim cell As Range
Selection.Value = Selection.Value

'Check each cell
For Each cell In Selection
'Extract the hour from it
With cell
.Value = Hour(cell)
.NumberFormat = "0"
End With
Next cell

End Sub
```

STEP 3: Let us test it out!

Open the sheet containing the data. Make sure your data is highlighted. Go to *Developer > Code > Macros*

Make sure your Macro is selected. Click **Run**.

With just one click, **all of your times are now converted to hours**!

Convert Time into Minutes

What does it do?

Convert your selected time into minute values

Copy Source Code:

```
'Make sure you have selected a range of cells first
Sub ConvertTimeIntoMinutes()
Dim cell As Range
Selection.Value = Selection.Value
'Check each cell
For Each cell In Selection
'Extract the minutes from it
With cell
.Value = Minute(cell)
.NumberFormat = "0"
End With
Next cell
End Sub
```

Final Result:

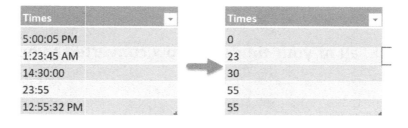

Macros are also capable of processing dates and times. Let us see how we can **convert time into minute values** using Excel Macros!

These are our times to convert:

Times
5:00:05 PM
1:23:45 AM
14:30:00
23:55
12:55:32 PM

STEP 1: Go to *Developer > Code > Visual Basic*

STEP 2: Paste in your code and **Select Save**. Close the window afterwards.

```vba
'Make sure you have selected a range of cells first
Sub ConvertTimeIntoMinutes()

Dim cell As Range
Selection.Value = Selection.Value

'Check each cell
For Each cell In Selection
'Extract the minutes from it
With cell
.Value = Minute(cell)
.NumberFormat = "0"
End With
Next cell

End Sub
```

STEP 3: Let us test it out!

Open the sheet containing the data. Make sure your data is highlighted. Go to *Developer > Code > Macros*

Visual Basic | Macros | Use Relative References | Macro Security | Add-ins | Excel Add-ins | COM Add-ins | Insert | Design Mode | Properties | View Code | Run Dialog | Source | Map Properties | Expansion Packs | Refresh Data | Import | Export

Code   Add-ins   Controls   XML

Make sure your Macro is selected. Click **Run**.

Macro   ?   ✕

Macro name:

Sheet1.ConvertTimeIntoMinutes

Sheet1.ConvertTimeIntoMinutes

Run

Step Into

Edit

Create

Delete

Options...

Macros in: All Open Workbooks

Description

Cancel

Times

Times
5:00:05 PM
1:23:45 AM
14:30:00
23:55
12:55:32 PM

With just one click, **all of your times are now converted to minutes**!

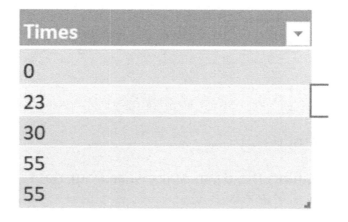

Times
0
23
30
55
55

Convert Time into Seconds

What does it do?

Convert your selected time into second values

Copy Source Code:

```
'Make sure you have selected a range of cells first
Sub ConvertTimeIntoSeconds()
Dim cell As Range
Selection.Value = Selection.Value
'Check each cell
For Each cell In Selection
'Extract the second from it
With cell
.Value = Second(cell)
.NumberFormat = "0"
End With
Next cell
End Sub
```

Final Result:

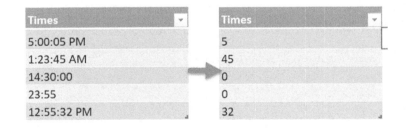

Macros are also capable of processing dates and times. Let us see how we can **convert time into second values** using Excel Macros!

These are our times to convert:

Times
5:00:05 PM
1:23:45 AM
14:30:00
23:55
12:55:32 PM

STEP 1: Go to *Developer > Code > Visual Basic*

STEP 2: Paste in your code and **Select Save**. Close the window afterwards.

```
'Make sure you have selected a range of cells first
Sub ConvertTimeIntoSeconds()

Dim cell As Range
Selection.Value = Selection.Value

'Check each cell
For Each cell In Selection
'Extract the second from it
With cell
.Value = Second(cell)
.NumberFormat = "0"
End With
Next cell

End Sub
```

STEP 3: Let us test it out!

Open the sheet containing the data. Make sure your data is highlighted. Go to *Developer > Code > Macros*

Visual Basic | Macros | Use Relative References | Macro Security | Add-ins | Excel Add-ins | COM Add-ins | Insert | Design Mode | Properties | View Code | Run Dialog | Source | Map Properties | Expansion Packs | Refresh Data | Import | Export

Code   Add-ins   Controls   XML

Make sure your Macro is selected. Click **Run**.

Macro   ?   ✕

Macro name:

Sheet1.ConvertTimeIntoSeconds ⬆ | **Run**

Sheet1.ConvertTimeIntoSeconds | Step Into

Edit

Create

Delete

Options...

Macros in: | All Open Workbooks

Description

Cancel

Times

| 5:00:05 PM |
| 1:23:45 AM |
| 14:30:00 |
| 23:55 |
| 12:55:32 PM |

With just one click, **all of your times are now converted to seconds**!

Times ▼

| 5 |
| 45 |
| 0 |
| 0 |
| 32 |

Convert UK Dates to US Dates

What does it do?

Convert your selected dates from UK Date Format to US Date Format

Copy Source Code:

```
'Make sure you have selected a range of cells first
Sub ConvertUkDatesToUsDates()

Selection.NumberFormat = "MMM-DD-YY"

End Sub
```

Final Result:

Do you recall having a scenario where your dates in Excel are using the incorrect format? You can **convert UK dates to US dates using Macros in Excel**!

With this tutorial we will be converting from UK format (e.g. 31/12/2020) to US format (e.g. 12/31/2020).

Here are our dates in UK Format:

Dates ▼
31-Jan-19
29-Feb-20
28-Mar-21
16-Apr-22
15-May-20

STEP 1: Go to *Developer > Code > Visual Basic*

STEP 2: Paste in your code and **Select Save**. Close the window afterwards.

```
'Make sure you have selected a range of cells first
Sub ConvertUkDatesToUsDates()

Selection.NumberFormat = "MMM-DD-YY"

End Sub
```

STEP 3: Let us test it out!

Open the sheet containing the data. Make sure your data is highlighted. Go to *Developer > Code > Macros*

Make sure your Macro is selected. Click **Run**.

With just one click, **all of your dates are now in the US format**!

Convert US Dates to UK Dates

What does it do?

Convert your selected dates from US Date Format to UK Date Format

Copy Source Code:

```
'Make sure you have selected a range of cells first
Sub ConvertUsDatesToUkDates()

Selection.NumberFormat = "DD-MMM-YY"

End Sub
```

Final Result:

Dates ▼
1/31/19
2/29/20
3/28/21
4/16/22
5/15/20

→

Dates ▼
31-Jan-19
29-Feb-20
28-Mar-21
16-Apr-22
15-May-20

Do you recall having a scenario where your dates in Excel are using the incorrect format? You can **convert US dates to UK dates using Macros in Excel**!

With this tutorial we will be converting from US format (e.g. 12/31/2020) to UK format (e.g. 31/12/2020).

Here are our dates in US Format:

Dates	▼
1/31/19	
2/29/20	
3/28/21	
4/16/22	
5/15/20	

STEP 1: Go to *Developer > Code > Visual Basic*

STEP 2: Paste in your code and **Select Save**. Close the window afterwards.

```
'Make sure you have selected a range of cells first
Sub ConvertUsDatesToUkDates()

Selection.NumberFormat = "DD-MMM-YY"

End Sub
```

STEP 3: Let us test it out!

Open the sheet containing the data. Make sure your data is highlighted. Go to *Developer > Code > Macros*

Make sure your Macro is selected. Click **Run**.

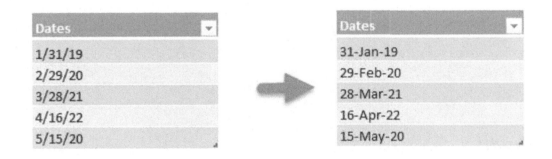

With just one click, **all of your dates are now in the UK format**!

Extract Number from Text

What does it do?

Creates a custom formula that extracts the numeric part from text

Copy Source Code:

```
'Create your own formula to retrieve the numeric portion of your
text
'Assumption is there is only one numeric portion in the text

Function GetNumericPart(CellRef As String)

Dim LengthOfText As Integer

LengthOfText = Len(CellRef)

'loop through each character, then append the numeric parts
together
Result = ""
For ctr = 1 To LengthOfText
If IsNumeric(Mid(CellRef, ctr, 1)) _
Then Result = Result & Mid(CellRef, ctr, 1)
Next ctr

GetNumericPart = Result

End Function
```

Final Result:

Sentences		Extracted Number
There are 15 dogs.		15
Number 100 is my favorite.		100
I ordered 50 shirts, where are they?	50	
The most I can eat are 3 burgers.		3
Have a lot of fun With 101 Macros!	101	

Want to create your own formula definition? You can do that using Excel Macros! Let us create a formula that **extracts the number from text**. The assumption here is there is only one number in your text to extract.

This is our text. Let us create our formula!

Sentences	Extracted Number
There are 15 dogs.	
Number 100 is my favorite.	
I ordered 50 shirts, where are they?	
The most I can eat are 3 burgers.	
Have a lot of fun With 101 Macros!	

STEP 1: Go to *Developer > Code > Visual Basic*

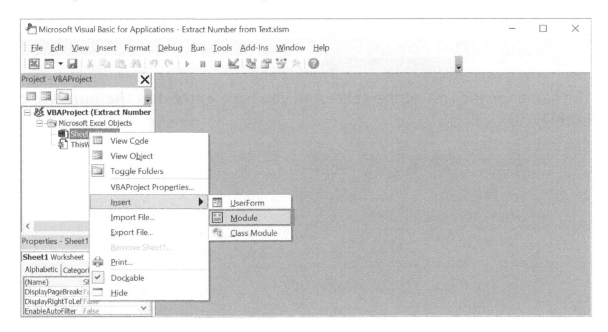

STEP 2: Right click on Sheet1 and go to *Insert > Module.*

Paste in your code and **Select Save**. Close the window afterwards.

```
Microsoft Visual Basic for Applications - Extract Number from Text.xlsm - [Module1 (Code)]

File  Edit  View  Insert  Format  Debug  Run  Tools  Add-Ins  Window  Help

(General)                                          GetNumericPart

'Create your own formula to retrieve the numeric portion of your text
'Assumption is there is only one numeric portion in the text

Function GetNumericPart(CellRef As String)

Dim LengthOfText As Integer

LengthOfText = Len(CellRef)

'loop through each character, then append the numeric parts together
Result = ""
For ctr = 1 To LengthOfText
If IsNumeric(Mid(CellRef, ctr, 1)) _
Then Result = Result & Mid(CellRef, ctr, 1)
Next ctr

GetNumericPart = Result

End Function
```

STEP 3: Let us test it out!

Open the sheet containing the data. Type in your new custom
formula: *=GetNumericPart(B8)*

Sentences	Extracted Number
There are 15 dogs.	=GetNumericPart(B8)
Number 100 is my favorite.	
I ordered 50 shirts, where are they?	
The most I can eat are 3 burgers.	
Have a lot of fun With 101 Macros!	

Do the same for the rest of the cells. And you have **extracted the numeric part using Macros**!

Sentences	Extracted Number
There are 15 dogs.	15
Number 100 is my favorite.	100
I ordered 50 shirts, where are they?	50
The most I can eat are 3 burgers.	3
Have a lot of fun With 101 Macros!	101

Format Values to Dollars and 2 Decimal Places

What does it do?

Format your selected values to dollars with 2 decimal places

Copy Source Code:

```
'Make sure you have a selection of numbers ready
Sub FormatValuesToDollars()
Dim rng As range
Selection.Value = Selection.Value
'Loop through the cells
For Each rng In Selection
'If it is a number, then format it to a dollar value with 2
decimal places
If WorksheetFunction.IsNumber(rng) Then rng.NumberFormat =
"$#,###.00"
Next rng
End Sub
```

Final Result:

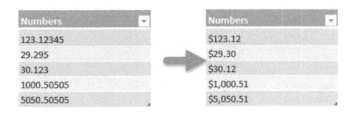

Have a bunch of values that you want to format as dollar values? You can do that easily through **Excel Macros**! You will be able format values to dollar with 2 decimal places.

These are our values:

Numbers	
123.12345	
29.295	
30.123	
1000.50505	
5050.50505	

STEP 1: Go to *Developer > Code > Visual Basic*

STEP 2: Paste in your code and **Select Save**. Close the window afterwards.

```vba
'Make sure you have a selection of numbers ready
Sub FormatValuesToDollars()

Dim rng As range

Selection.Value = Selection.Value

'Loop through the cells
For Each rng In Selection
'If it is a number, then format it to a dollar value with 2 decimal places
If WorksheetFunction.IsNumber(rng) Then rng.NumberFormat = "$#,###.00"
Next rng

End Sub
```

STEP 3: Let us test it out!

Open the sheet containing the data. Make sure your data is highlighted. Go to *Developer > Code > Macros*

Make sure your Macro is selected. Click **Run**.

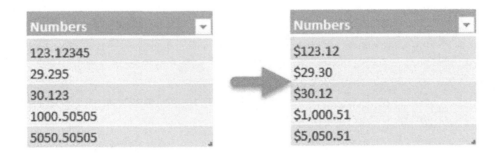

Macro		? ×
Macro name:		
Sheet1.FormatValuesToDollars ⬆		Run
Sheet1.FormatValuesToDollars		Step Into
		Edit
		Create
		Delete
		Options...
Macros in: All Open Workbooks		
Description		Cancel

Numbers
123.12345
29.295
30.123
1000.50505
5050.50505

With just one click, **all of your numbers are now formatted as dollars with 2 decimal places!**

Numbers		Numbers
123.12345		$123.12
29.295	→	$29.30
30.123		$30.12
1000.50505		$1,000.51
5050.50505		$5,050.51

Get Word Count from Worksheet

What does it do?

Displays the word count

Copy Source Code:

```
Sub GetWordCountFromWorksheet()

Dim totalCount As Long
Dim count As Long
Dim range As Range
Dim trimmedText As String

'Loop through all of the cells
For Each range In ActiveSheet.UsedRange.Cells
trimmedText = Application.WorksheetFunction.Trim(range.Text)
count = 0

'Count the number of words
If trimmedText <> vbNullString Then
count = Len(trimmedText) - Len(Replace(trimmedText, " ", "")) +
1
End If

totalCount = totalCount + count
Next range

MsgBox "There are a total of " & Format(totalCount, "#,##0") & "
words in the your worksheet"

End Sub
```

Final Result:

> **Microsoft Excel**   ✕
>
> There are a total of 8,765 words in the your worksheet
>
> OK

Wanted to count the number of words inside your spreadsheet? Excel Macros will **get the word count** for you!

This is our data table, let's check the number of words!

CUSTOMER	PRODUCTS	SALES PERSON	SALES REGION	ORDER DATE	SALES	FINANCIAL YEAR	SALES MONTH	SALES QTR	CHANNEL PARTNERS
LONG ISLANDS INC	SOFT DRINKS	Michael Jackson	AMERICAS	13/04/2012	24,640	2012	January	Q1	Acme, inc.
LONG ISLANDS INC	SOFT DRINKS	Michael Jackson	AMERICAS	21/12/2012	24,640	2012	February	Q1	Widget Corp
LONG ISLANDS INC	SOFT DRINKS	Michael Jackson	AMERICAS	24/12/2012	29,923	2012	March	Q1	123 Warehousing
LONG ISLANDS INC	SOFT DRINKS	Michael Jackson	AMERICAS	24/12/2012	66,901	2012	April	Q2	Demo Company
LONG ISLANDS INC	SOFT DRINKS	Michael Jackson	AMERICAS	29/12/2012	63,116	2012	May	Q2	Smith and Co.
LONG ISLANDS INC	SOFT DRINKS	Michael Jackson	AMERICAS	28/06/2012	38,281	2012	June	Q2	Foo Bars
LONG ISLANDS INC	SOFT DRINKS	Michael Jackson	AMERICAS	28/06/2012	57,650	2012	July	Q3	ABC Telecom
LONG ISLANDS INC	SOFT DRINKS	Michael Jackson	AMERICAS	29/06/2012	90,967	2012	August	Q3	Fake Brothers
LONG ISLANDS INC	SOFT DRINKS	Michael Jackson	AMERICAS	29/06/2012	11,910	2012	September	Q3	QWERTY Logistics
LONG ISLANDS INC	SOFT DRINKS	Michael Jackson	AMERICAS	06/07/2012	59,531	2012	October	Q4	Demo, inc.
LONG ISLANDS INC	SOFT DRINKS	Michael Jackson	AMERICAS	06/07/2012	88,297	2012	November	Q4	Sample Company
LONG ISLANDS INC	SOFT DRINKS	Michael Jackson	AMERICAS	08/09/2012	87,868	2012	December	Q4	Sample, inc
LONG ISLANDS INC	BOTTLES	Michael Jackson	AMERICAS	08/09/2012	95,527	2012	January	Q1	Acme Corp
LONG ISLANDS INC	BOTTLES	Michael Jackson	AMERICAS	30/06/2012	90,599	2012	February	Q1	Allied Biscuit
LONG ISLANDS INC	BOTTLES	Michael Jackson	AMERICAS	23/12/2012	17,030	2012	March	Q1	Ankh-Sto Associates
LONG ISLANDS INC	BOTTLES	Michael Jackson	AMERICAS	08/12/2012	65,026	2012	April	Q2	Extensive Enterprise
LONG ISLANDS INC	BOTTLES	Michael Jackson	AMERICAS	28/10/2012	57,579	2012	May	Q2	Galaxy Corp
LONG ISLANDS INC	BOTTLES	Michael Jackson	AMERICAS	28/10/2012	34,338	2012	June	Q2	Globo-Chem
LONG ISLANDS INC	BOTTLES	Michael Jackson	AMERICAS	15/09/2012	90,387	2012	July	Q3	Mr. Sparkle
LONG ISLANDS INC	BOTTLES	Michael Jackson	AMERICAS	28/10/2012	62,324	2012	August	Q3	Globex Corporation
LONG ISLANDS INC	BOTTLES	Michael Jackson	AMERICAS	31/10/2012	28,871	2012	September	Q3	LexCorp

Macro Data Table

STEP 1: Go to *Developer > Code > Visual Basic*

STEP 2: Paste in your code and **Select Save**. Close the window afterwards.

```
Sub GetWordCountFromWorksheet()

Dim totalCount As Long
Dim count As Long
Dim range As range
Dim trimmedText As String

'Loop through all of the cells
For Each range In ActiveSheet.UsedRange.Cells
trimmedText = Application.WorksheetFunction.Trim(range.Text)
count = 0

'Count the number of words
If trimmedText <> vbNullString Then
count = Len(trimmedText) - Len(Replace(trimmedText, " ", "")) + 1
End If

totalCount = totalCount + count
Next range

MsgBox "There are a total of " & Format(totalCount, "#,##0") & " words in the your worksheet"

End Sub
```

STEP 3: Let us test it out!

Open the sheet containing the data. Go to *Developer > Code > Macros*

Make sure your Macro is selected. Click **Run**.

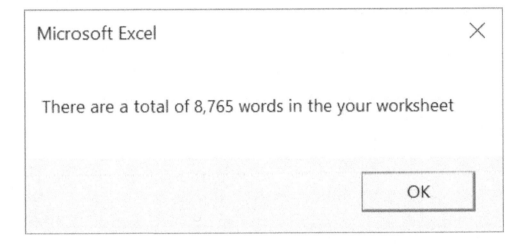

With just one click, **you now have displayed your word count**!

Microsoft Excel   ✕

There are a total of 8,765 words in the your worksheet

OK

Increase Cell Values by a Number

What does it do?

Add all selected values by a number

Copy Source Code:

```
'Make sure you have a range of values selected
Sub AddAllValuesByANumber()

Dim rng As Range
Dim num As Integer

num = InputBox("Enter your number to add to all", "Enter your
number")

'Loop through all of the values
For Each rng In Selection
'For each number, add it with the user input
If WorksheetFunction.IsNumber(rng) Then
rng.Value = rng + num
Else
End If
Next rng

End Sub
```

Final Result:

Numbers ▼
10
20
30
40
50

Numbers ▼
15
25
35
45
55

Let us have some fun and try to perform mathematical operations on a range of numbers. Let us try using Excel Macros to **add all values by a number**!

These are our numbers:

Numbers ▾
10
20
30
40
50

STEP 1: Go to *Developer > Code > Visual Basic*

STEP 2: Paste in your code and **Select Save**. Close the window afterwards.

```vba
'Make sure you have a range of values selected
Sub AddAllValuesByANumber()

Dim rng As range
Dim num As Integer

num = InputBox("Enter your number to add to all", "Enter your number")

'Loop through all of the values
For Each rng In Selection
'For each number, add it with the user input
If WorksheetFunction.IsNumber(rng) Then
rng.Value = rng + num
Else
End If
Next rng

End Sub
```

STEP 3: Let us test it out!

Open the sheet containing the data. Make sure your values are highlighted. Go to *Developer > Code > Macros*

Make sure your Macro is selected. Click **Run**.

Enter 5 to add all of them by 5. **Click OK.**

With just one click, **all of the values are now added by 5**!

Decrease Cell Values by a Number

What does it do?

Subtract all selected values by a number

Copy Source Code:

```
'Make sure you have a range of values selected
Sub SubtractAllValuesByANumber()

Dim rng As Range
Dim num As Integer

num = InputBox("Enter your number to subtract from all", "Enter
your number")

'Loop through all of the values
For Each rng In Selection
'For each number, subtract it from the user input
If WorksheetFunction.IsNumber(rng) Then
rng.Value = rng - num
Else
End If
Next rng

End Sub
```

Final Result:

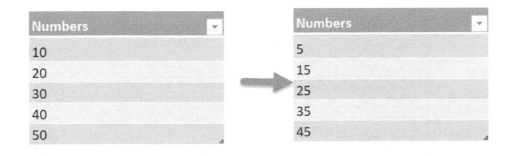

Let us have some fun and try to perform mathematical operations on a range of numbers. Let us try using Excel Macros to **subtract all values by a number**!

These are our numbers:

Numbers
10
20
30
40
50

STEP 1: Go to *Developer > Code > Visual Basic*

STEP 2: Paste in your code and **Select Save**. Close the window afterwards.

```
'Make sure you have a range of values selected
Sub SubtractAllValuesByANumber()

Dim rng As range
Dim num As Integer

num = InputBox("Enter your number to subtract from all", "Enter your number")

'Loop through all of the values
For Each rng In Selection
'For each number, subtract it from the user input
If WorksheetFunction.IsNumber(rng) Then
rng.Value = rng - num
Else
End If
Next rng

End Sub
```

STEP 3: Let us test it out!

Open the sheet containing the data. Make sure your values are highlighted. Go to *Developer > Code > Macros*

Make sure your Macro is selected. Click **Run**.

Enter 5 to subtract all of them by 5. **Click OK.**

With just one click, **all of the values are now subtracted by 5!**

Insert Time Range

What does it do?

Insert a time range by the hour from 1am to 12 midnight

Copy Source Code:

```
Sub InsertTimeRange()

Dim counter As Integer

'Insert the time range from 00:00 to 23:00
For counter = 1 To 24
ActiveCell.FormulaR1C1 = counter & ":00"
ActiveCell.NumberFormat = "[$-409]h:mm AM/PM;@"
'Move on to the next row
ActiveCell.Offset(RowOffset:=1, ColumnOffset:=0).Select
Next counter

End Sub
```

Final Result:

	A
6	1:00 AM
7	2:00 AM
8	3:00 AM
9	4:00 AM
10	5:00 AM
11	6:00 AM
12	7:00 AM
13	8:00 AM
14	9:00 AM
15	10:00 AM
16	11:00 AM
17	12:00 PM
18	1:00 PM
19	2:00 PM
20	3:00 PM
21	4:00 PM
22	5:00 PM
23	6:00 PM
24	7:00 PM
25	8:00 PM
26	9:00 PM
27	10:00 PM
28	11:00 PM
29	12:00 AM

Want to create a quick schedule and insert hourly times to your spreadsheet? You can use Excel Macros and looping to quickly **insert a time range from 1am all the way to 12 midnight**!

STEP 1: Go to *Developer > Code > Visual Basic*

STEP 2: Paste in your code and **Select Save**. Close the window afterwards.

```vba
Sub InsertTimeRange()

Dim counter As Integer

'Insert the time range from 00:00 to 23:00
For counter = 1 To 24
ActiveCell.FormulaR1C1 = counter & ":00"
ActiveCell.NumberFormat = "[$-409]h:mm AM/PM;@"
'Move on to the next row
ActiveCell.Offset(RowOffset:=1, ColumnOffset:=0).Select
Next counter

End Sub
```

STEP 3: Let us test it out!

Go to *Developer > Code > Macros*

Make sure your Macro is selected. Click **Run**.

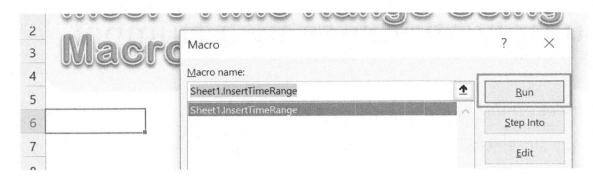

With just one click, **all hours are now generated**!

	A
6	1:00 AM
7	2:00 AM
8	3:00 AM
9	4:00 AM
10	5:00 AM
11	6:00 AM
12	7:00 AM
13	8:00 AM
14	9:00 AM
15	10:00 AM
16	11:00 AM
17	12:00 PM
18	1:00 PM
19	2:00 PM
20	3:00 PM
21	4:00 PM
22	5:00 PM
23	6:00 PM
24	7:00 PM
25	8:00 PM
26	9:00 PM
27	10:00 PM
28	11:00 PM
29	12:00 AM

Multiply all Values by a Number

What does it do?

Multiply all selected values by a number

Copy Source Code:

```
'Make sure you have a range of values selected
Sub MultiplyAllValuesByANumber()

Dim rng As Range
Dim num As Integer

num = InputBox("Enter your multiplier", "Enter your multiplier")

'Loop through all of the values
For Each rng In Selection
'For each number, multiply it with the user input
If WorksheetFunction.IsNumber(rng) Then
rng.Value = rng * num
Else
End If
Next rng

End Sub
```

Final Result:

Numbers	▼
10	
20	
30	
40	
50	

Numbers	▼
50	
100	
150	
200	
250	

Let us have some fun and try to perform mathematical operations on a range of numbers. Let us try using Excel Macros to **multiply all values by a number**!

These are our numbers:

Numbers
10
20
30
40
50

STEP 1: Go to *Developer > Code > Visual Basic*

STEP 2: Paste in your code and **Select Save**. Close the window afterwards.

```vba
'Make sure you have a range of values selected
Sub MultiplyAllValuesByANumber()

Dim rng As range
Dim num As Integer

num = InputBox("Enter your multiplier", "Enter your multiplier")

'Loop through all of the values
For Each rng In Selection
'For each number, multiply it with the user input
If WorksheetFunction.IsNumber(rng) Then
rng.Value = rng * num
Else
End If
Next rng

End Sub
```

STEP 3: Let us test it out!

Open the sheet containing the data. Make sure your values are highlighted. Go to *Developer > Code > Macros*

Make sure your Macro is selected. Click **Run**.

Enter 5 as the multiplier to multiply all of them by 5. **Click OK.**

With just one click, **all of the values are now multiplied by 5**!

Remove a Character from Selection

What does it do?

Remove your specified character from the selection of text

Copy Source Code:

```
Sub RemoveCharacterFromSelection()

Dim range As Range
Dim characters As String
'Get the characters to be removed from the user
characters = InputBox("Input the characters to remove", "Input
Characters to be removed")
'Replace it with blank
For Each range In Selection
range.Replace What:=characters, Replacement:=""
Next

End Sub
```

Final Result:

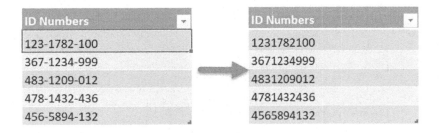

Excel has a feature of Find and Replace if you want to remove a character then replace it with a blank value. You can create your own functionality using Excel Macros! Let us aim to **remove a character from a selection of text** using Macros.

We have this list of ID Numbers, let us aim to remove the dashes (-) from them:

ID Numbers ▼
123-1782-100
367-1234-999
483-1209-012
478-1432-436
456-5894-132

STEP 1: Go to *Developer > Code > Visual Basic*

STEP 2: Paste in your code and **Select Save**. Close the window afterwards.

```
Sub RemoveCharacterFromSelection()

Dim range As range
Dim characters As String

'Get the characters to be removed from the user
characters = InputBox("Input the characters to remove", "Input Characters to be removed")

'Replace it with blank
For Each range In Selection
range.Replace What:=characters, Replacement:=""
Next

End Sub
```

STEP 3: Let us test it out!

Open the sheet containing the data. Make sure your id numbers are highlighted. Go to *Developer > Code > Macros*

Make sure your Macro is selected. Click **Run**.

Type in the dash (-) to have it removed. **Click OK.**

With just one click, **you have removed all of the dashes**!

ID Numbers
1231782100
3671234999
4831209012
4781432436
4565894132

Remove Apostrophe from Numbers

What does it do?

Removes apostrophe in front of numbers in your selection

Copy Source Code:

```
'If you have an apostrophe before your numbers, use this to
remove them
'Make sure you have selected a range of numbers
Sub RemoveApostropheFromNumbers()

Selection.Value = Selection.Value

End Sub
```

Final Result:

Sometimes we receive spreadsheets where the numbers have an apostrophe in front of them so that it gets treated as text. But what if we do not want that? Excel Macros will **remove apostrophe from numbers** in a single click!

Here are our numbers with apostrophes in front of them:

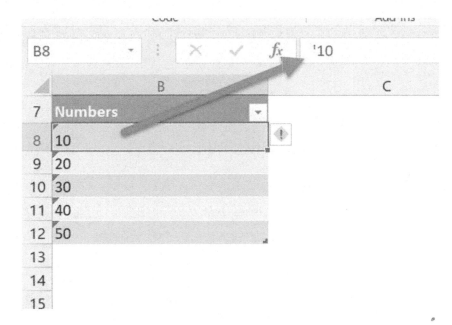

STEP 1: Go to *Developer > Code > Visual Basic*

STEP 2: Paste in your code and **Select Save**. Close the window afterwards.

```
'If you have an apostrophe before your numbers, use this to remove them
'Make sure you have selected a range of numbers
Sub RemoveApostropheFromNumbers()

Selection.Value = Selection.Value

End Sub
```

STEP 3: Let us test it out!

Open the sheet containing the data. Make sure your numbers are highlighted.
Go to *Developer > Code > Macros*

Make sure your Macro is selected. Click **Run**.

With just one click, **all of the apostrophes are now removed**!

Remove Characters at the Start

What does it do?

Removes the number of characters at the start as specified by the user

Copy Source Code:

```
Sub RemoveCharactersAtTheStart()

Dim range As Range
Dim num As Integer

'Get the characters to be removed from the user
num = InputBox("Input the number of characters to remove at the
start", "Num of characters")

'Loop through all of the text
For Each range In Selection
'Use Right to remove the first x characters
range = Right(range, Len(range) - num)
Next range

End Sub
```

Final Result:

PART #
2-19281013x
5-20767748a
k-46612687d
0-10017191y
9-34793800d
k-46677751e

PART #
19281013x
20767748a
46612687d
10017191y
34793800d
46677751e

Want to quickly truncate the first number of characters of your choosing? Excel Macros can remove characters at the start of your selection of text!

This is the text that we want to modify. We want to remove the first 2 characters of these Part Numbers:

PART #
2-19281013x
5-20767748a
k-46612687d
0-10017191y
9-34793800d
k-46677751e

STEP 1: Go to *Developer > Code > Visual Basic*

STEP 2: Paste in your code and **Select Save**. Close the window afterwards.

STEP 3: Let us test it out!

Open the sheet containing the data. Make sure your part numbers are highlighted. Go to *Developer > Code > Macros*

Make sure your Macro is selected. Click **Run**.

We want to remove the first 2 characters. Type in 2 and **Click OK**.

With just one click, **the first 2 characters are now all removed**!

PART #
19281013x
20767748a
46612687d
10017191y
34793800d
46677751e

Remove Date from Date and Time

What does it do?

Removes the date component from your date time

Copy Source Code:

```
'Make sure you have a range of cells selected
Sub RemoveDateFromDateTime()
Dim cell As Range
'Loop through all of the cells
For Each cell In Selection
If IsDate(cell) = True Then
cell.Value = cell.Value - VBA.Fix(cell.Value)
End If
Next
'Change it to a time format
Selection.NumberFormat = "hh:mm:ss am/pm"
End Sub
```

Final Result:

Have a bunch of date times, and you want to keep the time only? You can **remove date from the date and time** using Excel Macros in a single click!

Here is our list of dates and times:

Date Time	
01/01/2019 17:00	
02/02/2020 1:23	
03/03/2021 14:30	
04/04/2022 23:55	
05/05/2023 12:55	

STEP 1: Go to *Developer > Code > Visual Basic*

STEP 2: Paste in your code and **Select Save**. Close the window afterwards.

```vba
'Make sure you have a range of cells selected
Sub RemoveDateFromDateTime()

Dim cell As Range

'Loop through all of the cells
For Each cell In Selection
If IsDate(cell) = True Then
cell.Value = cell.Value - VBA.Fix(cell.Value)
End If
Next

'Change it to a time format
Selection.NumberFormat = "hh:mm:ss am/pm"

End Sub
```

STEP 3: Let us test it out!

Open the sheet containing the data. Make sure your date times are highlighted.
Go to *Developer > Code > Macros*

Make sure your Macro is selected. Click **Run**.

With just one click, **all of the dates from the date times are now removed**!

Date Time	
05:00:05 PM	
01:23:45 AM	
02:30:00 PM	
11:55:00 PM	
12:55:32 PM	

Remove Time from Date and Time

What does it do?

Removes the time component from your dates

Copy Source Code:

```
'Make sure you have a range of cells selected
Sub RemoveTimeFromDateTime()
Dim cell As Range
'Loop through all of the cells
For Each cell In Selection
If IsDate(cell) = True Then
cell.Value = VBA.Int(cell.Value)
End If
Next
'Change it to a date format
Selection.NumberFormat = "mmm-dd-yy"
End Sub
```

Final Result:

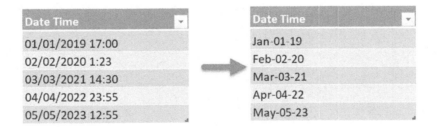

Wanted to make your date times simpler by removing the time component?
Excel Macros make it possible to **remove the time from dates** easily!

This is our list of dates with times:

Date Time ▾
01/01/2019 17:00
02/02/2020 1:23
03/03/2021 14:30
04/04/2022 23:55
05/05/2023 12:55

STEP 1: Go to *Developer > Code > Visual Basic*

STEP 2: Paste in your code and **Select Save**. Close the window afterwards.

```
'Make sure you have a range of cells selected
Sub RemoveTimeFromDateTime()

Dim cell As Range

'Loop through all of the cells
For Each cell In Selection
If IsDate(cell) = True Then
cell.Value = VBA.Int(cell.Value)
End If
Next

'Change it to a date format
Selection.NumberFormat = "mmm-dd-yy"

End Sub
```

STEP 3: Let us test it out!

Open the sheet containing the data. Make sure your date times are highlighted.
Go to *Developer > Code > Macros*

Make sure your Macro is selected. Click **Run**.

With just one click, **all of the times from the dates are now removed**!

Date Time	
Jan-01-19	
Feb-02-20	
Mar-03-21	
Apr-04-22	
May-05-23	

Remove Decimals from Numbers

What does it do?

Removes the decimal component from your selected numbers

Copy Source Code:

```
'Make sure you have a selection ready
Sub RemoveDecimalsFromNumbers()
Dim rng As Range
'Loop through the selection
For Each rng In Selection
If WorksheetFunction.IsNumber(rng) Then
'Convert it to an integer to remove the decimal portion
rng.Value= Int(rng)
rng.NumberFormat= "0"
Else
End If
Next rng
End Sub
```

Final Result:

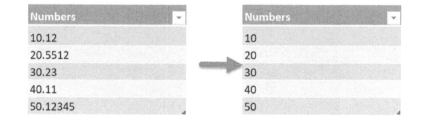

Have a lot of numbers and you want to completely remove the decimal portions? Excel Macros can **remove decimals from numbers** in a single click!

Here are our numbers:

Numbers	
10.12	
20.5512	
30.23	
40.11	
50.12345	

STEP 1: Go to *Developer > Code > Visual Basic*

STEP 2: Paste in your code and **Select Save**. Close the window afterwards.

```
'Make sure you have a selection ready
Sub RemoveDecimalsFromNumbers()

Dim rng As range

'Loop through the selection
For Each rng In Selection
If WorksheetFunction.IsNumber(rng) Then
'Convert it to an integer to remove the decimal portion
rng.Value = Int(rng)
rng.NumberFormat = "0"
Else
End If
Next rng

End Sub
```

STEP 3: Let us test it out!

Open the sheet containing the data. Make sure your numbers are highlighted.
Go to *Developer > Code > Macros*

Make sure your Macro is selected. Click **Run**.

With just one click, **all of the decimal components are now removed**!

Replace Blanks with Zeros

What does it do?

Replaces blanks with zeros in your selection

Copy Source Code:

```
'Make sure you have a selection ready
Sub ReplaceBlanksWithZeros()

Dim range As Range

Selection.Value= Selection.Value

'Loop through all the cells
For Each range In Selection
'If it is a blank or one space, then replace it with 0
If range = "" Or range = " " Then
range.Value= "0"
Else
End If
Next range

End Sub
```

Final Result:

PRODUCTS	SALES REGION	ORDER DATE	SALES
SOFT DRINKS	AMERICAS	06/07/2012	88,297
SOFT DRINKS	AMERICAS	08/09/2012	
BOTTLES	AMERICAS	08/09/2012	95,527
BOTTLES	AMERICAS	30/06/2012	90,599
BOTTLES	AMERICAS	08/12/2012	
ICE CUBES	AMERICAS	01/12/2012	
ICE CUBES	AMERICAS	01/12/2012	34,096
ICE CUBES	AMERICAS	28/10/2012	
ICE CUBES	AMERICAS	19/08/2012	15,306
ICE CUBES	AMERICAS	08/02/2012	11,347

PRODUCTS	SALES REGION	ORDER DATE	SALES
SOFT DRINKS	AMERICAS	06/07/2012	88,297
SOFT DRINKS	AMERICAS	08/09/2012	0
BOTTLES	AMERICAS	08/09/2012	95,527
BOTTLES	AMERICAS	30/06/2012	90,599
BOTTLES	AMERICAS	08/12/2012	0
ICE CUBES	AMERICAS	01/12/2012	0
ICE CUBES	AMERICAS	01/12/2012	34,096
ICE CUBES	AMERICAS	28/10/2012	0
ICE CUBES	AMERICAS	19/08/2012	15,306
ICE CUBES	AMERICAS	08/02/2012	11,347

It is so common for me to have a column of numbers with blanks. But it would be more readable for me to **replace blanks with zeros** instead. Excel Macros can do this for us!

This is our list of values, see that the Sales column has blanks:

	PRODUCTS	SALES REGION	ORDER DATE	SALES
7	SOFT DRINKS	AMERICAS	06/07/2012	88,297
8	SOFT DRINKS	AMERICAS	08/09/2012	
9	BOTTLES	AMERICAS	08/09/2012	95,527
0	BOTTLES	AMERICAS	30/06/2012	90,599
1	BOTTLES	AMERICAS	08/12/2012	
2	ICE CUBES	AMERICAS	01/12/2012	
3	ICE CUBES	AMERICAS	01/12/2012	34,096
4	ICE CUBES	AMERICAS	28/10/2012	
5	ICE CUBES	AMERICAS	19/08/2012	15,306
6	ICE CUBES	AMERICAS	08/02/2012	11,347
7				

STEP 1: Go to *Developer > Code > Visual Basic*

STEP 2: Paste in your code and **Select Save**. Close the window afterwards.

```vba
'Make sure you have a selection ready
Sub ReplaceBlanksWithZeros()

Dim range As range

Selection.Value = Selection.Value

'Loop through all the cells
For Each range In Selection
'If it is a blank or one space, then replace it with 0
If range = "" Or range = " " Then
range.Value = "0"
Else
End If
Next range

End Sub
```

STEP 3: Let us test it out!

Open the sheet containing the data. Make sure your sales column is highlighted. Go to *Developer > Code > Macros*

Make sure your Macro is selected. Click **Run**.

With just one click, **all of the blanks are now replaced with zeros**!

PRODUCTS	SALES REGION	ORDER DATE	SALES
SOFT DRINKS	AMERICAS	06/07/2012	88,297
SOFT DRINKS	AMERICAS	08/09/2012	0
BOTTLES	AMERICAS	08/09/2012	95,527
BOTTLES	AMERICAS	30/06/2012	90,599
BOTTLES	AMERICAS	08/12/2012	0
ICE CUBES	AMERICAS	01/12/2012	0
ICE CUBES	AMERICAS	01/12/2012	34,096
ICE CUBES	AMERICAS	28/10/2012	0
ICE CUBES	AMERICAS	19/08/2012	15,306
ICE CUBES	AMERICAS	08/02/2012	11,347

Trim Extra Spaces from Selection

What does it do?

Removes spaces at the start and end from your selection

Copy Source Code:

```
Sub RemoveExtraSpacesFromSelection()
Dim range As Range
Dim cell As Range
Set range = Selection
'loop through each cell and trim them
For Each cell In range
If Not IsEmpty(cell) Then
cell = Trim(cell)
End If
Next cell
End Sub
```

Final Result:

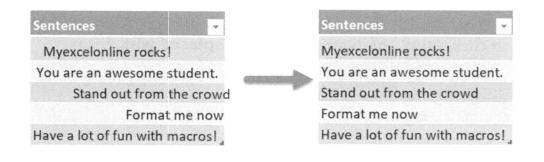

If you want to quickly **remove extra spaces at the start and end of your text**, Excel Macros will do that for you! It is very similar to the TRIM formula as well.

These are our text that we want to clean up:

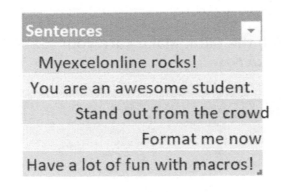

Sentences
Myexcelonline rocks!
You are an awesome student.
Stand out from the crowd
Format me now
Have a lot of fun with macros!

STEP 1: Go to *Developer > Code > Visual Basic*

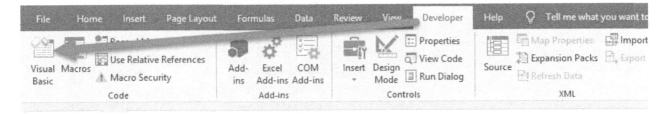

STEP 2: Paste in your code and **Select Save**. Close the window afterwards.

```vba
Sub RemoveExtraSpacesFromSelection()

Dim range As range
Dim cell As range

Set range = Selection

'loop through each cell and trim them
For Each cell In range
If Not IsEmpty(cell) Then
cell = Trim(cell)
End If
Next cell

End Sub
```

STEP 3: Let us test it out!

Open the sheet containing the data. Make sure your text is highlighted. Go to *Developer > Code > Macros*

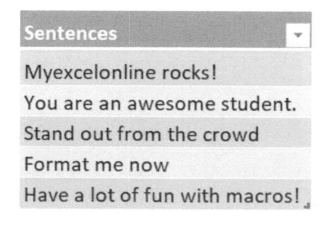

Make sure your Macro is selected. Click **Run**.

With just one click, **all of the unneeded extra spaces are all removed**!

HIGHLIGHTING MACROS

Highlight Active Row & Column

What does it do?

Highlights the Active Row and Column By the Double Click

Copy Source Code:

```
Private Sub Worksheet_BeforeDoubleClick(ByVal Target As range,
Cancel As Boolean)

Dim selection As String

'Generate the Range that contains the current column and row
selection = Target.Cells.Address & "," & _
Target.Cells.EntireColumn.Address & "," & _
Target.Cells.EntireRow.Address

'Select that range
Range(selection).Select
End Sub
```

Final Result:

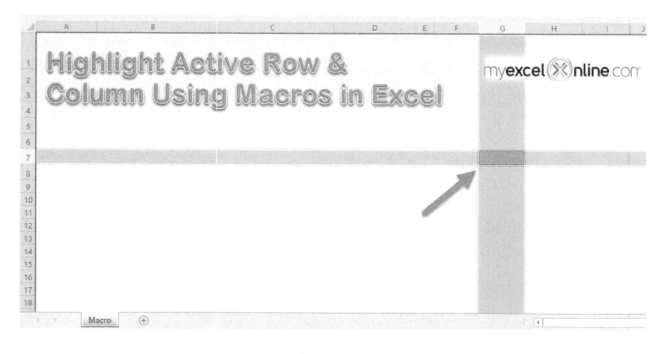

We have a cool trick to show you using Macros, you can **highlight the active row and column** by double clicking!

Do take note that this will override your original double click behavior.

STEP 1: Go to **Developer > Code > Visual Basic**

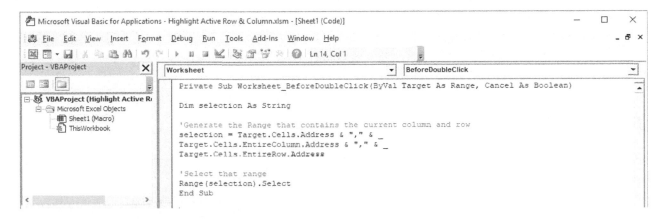

STEP 2: Paste in your code and **Select Save**. Close the window afterwards.

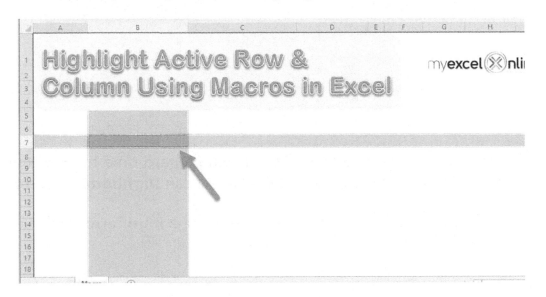

STEP 3: Let us test it out!

Just double click anywhere, and it will **highlight the active row and column!**

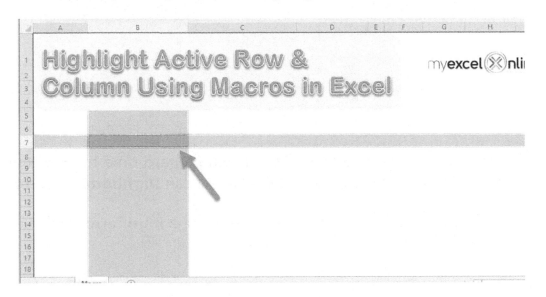

Highlight All Errors with a Red Color

What does it do?

Highlight all of the errors

Copy Source Code:

```
Sub HighlightAllErrors()
Dim cell As Range
For Each cell In ActiveSheet.UsedRange
'Check if it is an error, then change the style to be Bad
If WorksheetFunction.IsError(cell) Then
cell.Style = "Bad"
End If
Next cell
End Sub
```

Final Result:

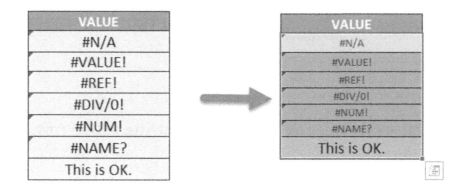

Have a lot of errors in your worksheet but having a hard time finding them? Excel Macros will make short work of this and we can **highlight all errors**!

Here is our initial set of data, you can see there are a lot of errors in there:

VALUE
#N/A
#VALUE!
#REF!
#DIV/0!
#NUM!
#NAME?
This is OK.

STEP 1: Go to *Developer > Code > Visual Basic*

STEP 2: Paste in your code and **Select Save**. Close the window afterwards.

```
Sub HighlightAllErrors()

Dim cell As Range

For Each cell In ActiveSheet.UsedRange
'Check if it is an error, then change the style to be Bad
If WorksheetFunction.IsError(cell) Then
cell.Style = "Bad"
End If
Next cell

End Sub
```

STEP 3: Let us test it out!

Open the sheet containing the data. Go to *Developer > Code > Macros*

Make sure your Macro is selected. Click **Run**.

With just one click, **all of the cells with errors are now highlighted!**

Highlight All Named Ranges

What does it do?

Highlight all Named Ranges

Copy Source Code:

```
Sub HighlightAllNamedRanges()

Dim RangeName As Name
Dim SelectedRange As Range
On Error Resume Next
'Loop through all named ranges
For Each RangeName In ActiveWorkbook.Names
Set SelectedRange = RangeName.RefersToRange
'Highlight with the color yellow
SelectedRange.Interior.ColorIndex = 27
Next RangeName
End Sub
```

Final Result:

	PRODUCTS		SALES REGION	DATE	
LONG ISLANDS INC	SOFT DRINKS	Michael Jackson	AMERICAS	4/13/2012	24,640
LONG ISLANDS INC	SOFT DRINKS	Michael Jackson	AMERICAS	12/21/2012	24,640
LONG ISLANDS INC	SOFT DRINKS	Michael Jackson	AMERICAS	12/24/2012	29,923
LONG ISLANDS INC	SOFT DRINKS	Michael Jackson	AMERICAS	12/24/2012	66,901
LONG ISLANDS INC	SOFT DRINKS	Michael Jackson	AMERICAS	12/29/2012	63,116
TEQUILA TACOS LTD	SOFT DRINKS	John Michaloudis	ASIA	7/14/2012	46,063
TEQUILA TACOS LTD	SOFT DRINKS	John Michaloudis	ASIA	5/12/2012	95,529
TEQUILA TACOS LTD	SOFT DRINKS	John Michaloudis	ASIA	5/12/2012	27,946
TEQUILA TACOS LTD	BOTTLES	John Michaloudis	ASIA	8/23/2012	48,278
TEQUILA TACOS LTD	BOTTLES	John Michaloudis	ASIA	2/1/2012	70,149
LONG ISLANDS INC	SOFT DRINKS	Michael Jackson	AMERICAS	7/6/2012	88,297

If you have a lot of named ranges in your worksheet, and you want to see which ones are there quickly? You can quickly **highlight all named ranges** using Excel Macros!

For our example, these columns over here have **named ranges** defined.

CUSTOMER	PRODUCTS	SALES PERSON	SALES REGION	DATE	SALES
LONG ISLANDS INC	SOFT DRINKS	Michael Jackson	AMERICAS	4/13/2012	24,640
LONG ISLANDS INC	SOFT DRINKS	Michael Jackson	AMERICAS	12/21/2012	24,640
LONG ISLANDS INC	SOFT DRINKS	Michael Jackson	AMERICAS	12/24/2012	29,923
LONG ISLANDS INC	SOFT DRINKS	Michael Jackson	AMERICAS	12/24/2012	66,901
LONG ISLANDS INC	SOFT DRINKS	Michael Jackson	AMERICAS	12/29/2012	63,116
TEQUILA TACOS LTD	SOFT DRINKS	John Michaloudis	ASIA	7/14/2012	46,063
TEQUILA TACOS LTD	SOFT DRINKS	John Michaloudis	ASIA	5/12/2012	95,529
TEQUILA TACOS LTD	SOFT DRINKS	John Michaloudis	ASIA	5/12/2012	27,946
TEQUILA TACOS LTD	BOTTLES	John Michaloudis	ASIA	8/23/2012	48,278
TEQUILA TACOS LTD	BOTTLES	John Michaloudis	ASIA	2/1/2012	70,149
LONG ISLANDS INC	SOFT DRINKS	Michael Jackson	AMERICAS	7/6/2012	88,297

Here are the named ranges, you can quickly view them via *Formulas > Defined Names > Name Manager*:

STEP 1: Go to *Developer > Code > Visual Basic*

STEP 2: Paste in your code and **Select Save**. Close the window afterwards.

```vba
Sub HighlightAllNamedRanges()

Dim RangeName As Name
Dim SelectedRange As Range
On Error Resume Next

'Loop through all named ranges
For Each RangeName In ActiveWorkbook.Names
Set SelectedRange = RangeName.RefersToRange

'Highlight with the color yellow
SelectedRange.Interior.ColorIndex = 27
Next RangeName

End Sub
```

STEP 3: Let us test it out!

Open the sheet containing the data. Go to *Developer > Code > Macros*

Make sure your Macro is selected. Click **Run**.

With just one click, **all of the named ranges are now highlighted**!

	PRODUCTS		SALES REGION	DATE	
LONG ISLANDS INC	SOFT DRINKS	Michael Jackson	AMERICAS	4/13/2012	24,640
LONG ISLANDS INC	SOFT DRINKS	Michael Jackson	AMERICAS	12/21/2012	24,640
LONG ISLANDS INC	SOFT DRINKS	Michael Jackson	AMERICAS	12/24/2012	29,923
LONG ISLANDS INC	SOFT DRINKS	Michael Jackson	AMERICAS	12/24/2012	66,901
LONG ISLANDS INC	SOFT DRINKS	Michael Jackson	AMERICAS	12/29/2012	63,116
TEQUILA TACOS LTD	SOFT DRINKS	John Michaloudis	ASIA	7/14/2012	46,063
TEQUILA TACOS LTD	SOFT DRINKS	John Michaloudis	ASIA	5/12/2012	95,529
TEQUILA TACOS LTD	SOFT DRINKS	John Michaloudis	ASIA	5/12/2012	27,946
TEQUILA TACOS LTD	BOTTLES	John Michaloudis	ASIA	8/23/2012	48,278
TEQUILA TACOS LTD	BOTTLES	John Michaloudis	ASIA	2/1/2012	70,149
LONG ISLANDS INC	SOFT DRINKS	Michael Jackson	AMERICAS	7/6/2012	88,297

Highlight Alternate Rows in Selection

What does it do?

Highlights alternate rows in your selection

Copy Source Code:

```
Sub HighlightAlternateRowsInSelection()
Dim range As Range
For Each range In Selection.Rows
'Check if it's the alternate row by using modulo, set it to the
style of note
If range.Row Mod 2 = 1 Then
range.Style = "Note"
Else
End If
Next range
End Sub
```

Final Result:

CUSTOMER	PRODUCTS	SALES PERSON	SALES REGION	DATE	SALES
LONG ISLANDS INC	SOFT DRINKS	Michael Jackson	AMERICAS	41012	24640
LONG ISLANDS INC	SOFT DRINKS	Michael Jackson	AMERICAS	41264	24640
LONG ISLANDS INC	SOFT DRINKS	Michael Jackson	AMERICAS	41267	29923
LONG ISLANDS INC	SOFT DRINKS	Michael Jackson	AMERICAS	41267	66901
LONG ISLANDS INC	SOFT DRINKS	Michael Jackson	AMERICAS	41272	63116
TEQUILA TACOS LTD	SOFT DRINKS	John Michaloudis	ASIA	41104	46063
TEQUILA TACOS LTD	SOFT DRINKS	John Michaloudis	ASIA	41041	95529
TEQUILA TACOS LTD	SOFT DRINKS	John Michaloudis	ASIA	41041	27946
TEQUILA TACOS LTD	BOTTLES	John Michaloudis	ASIA	41144	48278
TEQUILA TACOS LTD	BOTTLES	John Michaloudis	ASIA	40940	70149
LONG ISLANDS INC	SOFT DRINKS	Michael Jackson	AMERICAS	41096	88297

CUSTOMER	PRODUCTS	SALES PERSON	SALES REGION	DATE	SALES
LONG ISLANDS INC	SOFT DRINKS	Michael Jackson	AMERICAS	41012	24640
LONG ISLANDS INC	SOFT DRINKS	Michael Jackson	AMERICAS	41264	24640
LONG ISLANDS INC	SOFT DRINKS	Michael Jackson	AMERICAS	41267	29923
LONG ISLANDS INC	SOFT DRINKS	Michael Jackson	AMERICAS	41267	66901
LONG ISLANDS INC	SOFT DRINKS	Michael Jackson	AMERICAS	41272	63116
TEQUILA TACOS LTD	SOFT DRINKS	John Michaloudis	ASIA	41104	46063
TEQUILA TACOS LTD	SOFT DRINKS	John Michaloudis	ASIA	41041	95529
TEQUILA TACOS LTD	SOFT DRINKS	John Michaloudis	ASIA	41041	27946
TEQUILA TACOS LTD	BOTTLES	John Michaloudis	ASIA	41144	48278
TEQUILA TACOS LTD	BOTTLES	John Michaloudis	ASIA	40940	70149
LONG ISLANDS INC	SOFT DRINKS	Michael Jackson	AMERICAS	41096	88297

When it comes to highlighting alternate rows in your data, it's a cumbersome process! One way is to use the table formatting option in Excel, but you can also use Excel Macros to **highlight alternate rows** for you!

And you have full control on how it will look like!

Here is our initial set of data:

CUSTOMER	PRODUCTS	SALES PERSON	SALES REGION	DATE	SALES
LONG ISLANDS INC	SOFT DRINKS	Michael Jackson	AMERICAS	41012	24640
LONG ISLANDS INC	SOFT DRINKS	Michael Jackson	AMERICAS	41264	24640
LONG ISLANDS INC	SOFT DRINKS	Michael Jackson	AMERICAS	41267	29923
LONG ISLANDS INC	SOFT DRINKS	Michael Jackson	AMERICAS	41267	66901
LONG ISLANDS INC	SOFT DRINKS	Michael Jackson	AMERICAS	41272	63116
TEQUILA TACOS LTD	SOFT DRINKS	John Michaloudis	ASIA	41104	46063
TEQUILA TACOS LTD	SOFT DRINKS	John Michaloudis	ASIA	41041	95529
TEQUILA TACOS LTD	SOFT DRINKS	John Michaloudis	ASIA	41041	27946
TEQUILA TACOS LTD	BOTTLES	John Michaloudis	ASIA	41144	48278
TEQUILA TACOS LTD	BOTTLES	John Michaloudis	ASIA	40940	70149
LONG ISLANDS INC	SOFT DRINKS	Michael Jackson	AMERICAS	41096	88297

STEP 1: Go to *Developer > Code > Visual Basic*

STEP 2: Paste in your code and **Select Save**. Close the window afterwards.

```
Sub HighlightAlternateRowsInSelection()

Dim range As range
For Each range In Selection.Rows

'Check if it's the alternate row by using modulo, set it to the style of note
If range.Row Mod 2 = 1 Then
range.Style = "Note"
Else
End If

Next range
End Sub
```

STEP 3: Let us test it out!

Open the sheet containing the data. Make sure your data is highlighted. Go to *Developer > Code > Macros*

Make sure your Macro is selected. Click **Run**.

With just one click, **the alternate rows of your selection are now highlighted**!

CUSTOMER	PRODUCTS	SALES PERSON	SALES REGION	DATE	SALES
LONG ISLANDS INC	SOFT DRINKS	Michael Jackson	AMERICAS	41012	24640
LONG ISLANDS INC	SOFT DRINKS	Michael Jackson	AMERICAS	41264	24640
LONG ISLANDS INC	SOFT DRINKS	Michael Jackson	AMERICAS	41267	29923
LONG ISLANDS INC	SOFT DRINKS	Michael Jackson	AMERICAS	41267	66901
LONG ISLANDS INC	SOFT DRINKS	Michael Jackson	AMERICAS	41272	63116
TEQUILA TACOS LTD	SOFT DRINKS	John Michaloudis	ASIA	41104	46063
TEQUILA TACOS LTD	SOFT DRINKS	John Michaloudis	ASIA	41041	95529
TEQUILA TACOS LTD	SOFT DRINKS	John Michaloudis	ASIA	41041	27946
TEQUILA TACOS LTD	BOTTLES	John Michaloudis	ASIA	41144	48278
TEQUILA TACOS LTD	BOTTLES	John Michaloudis	ASIA	40940	70149
LONG ISLANDS INC	SOFT DRINKS	Michael Jackson	AMERICAS	41096	88297

Highlight and Count a Specified Value

What does it do?

Highlight and show the count of a specified value

Copy Source Code:

```vba
Sub HighlightAndCountSpecifiedValue()

Dim cell As Range
Dim counter As Integer
Dim specificValue As Variant

'Get the specific value from the user
specificValue = InputBox("Enter Value To Highlight", "Enter
Value")

For Each cell In ActiveSheet.UsedRange

'If it matches the specified value, then change the style to be
Note
If cell = specificValue Then
cell.Style = "Note"
counter = counter + 1
End If
Next cell

'Show the total count to the user
MsgBox "There are a total of " & counter &" "& specificValue & "
in this worksheet."

End Sub
```

Final Result:

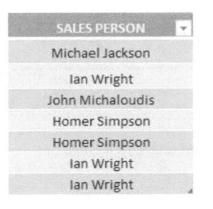

Let us try something fun using Excel Macros. We want to **highlight a specified value from the user, then show the count as well**! You will learn how to show a message back as well to your Excel user.

This is our initial set of data:

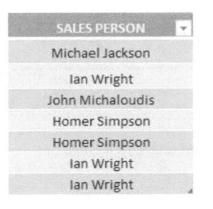

STEP 1: Go to *Developer > Code > Visual Basic*

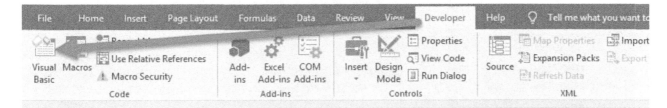

STEP 2: Paste in your code and **Select Save**. Close the window afterwards.

STEP 3: Let us test it out!

Open the sheet containing the data. Go to ***Developer > Code > Macros***

Make sure your Macro is selected. Click **Run**.

Type in the value to highlight and count. Let us type in **Ian Wright**. Click **OK**.

Enter Value	×
Enter Value To Highlight	OK
	Cancel
Ian Wright|	

With just one click, **all of the Ian Wright values are now highlighted and you see the count as well!**

SALES PERSON ▼
Michael Jackson
Ian Wright
John Michaloudis
Homer Simpson
Homer Simpson
Ian Wright
Ian Wright

Microsoft Excel	×
There are a total of 3 Ian Wright in this worksheet.	
	OK

Highlight Cells with a Single Space

What does it do?

Highlights all cells with a single space

Copy Source Code:

```
Sub HighlightTheSingleSpaces()

Dim range As Range

For Each range In ActiveSheet.UsedRange
'Check if it's a single space, then change the style to be Note
If range.Value = " " Then
range.Style = "Note"
End If
Next range

End Sub
```

Final Result:

VALUES ▼
549
682
376
-695
-625
561
-860
-838
-466

If you had a spreadsheet with a lot of single spaces, it is very annoying because it is hard to see. You can use Excel Macros to **highlight cells with a single space** easily!

This is our initial set of data, the ones enclosed in red are the ones with a single space (although it is not visible at an initial glance).

Double click in the empty cells and press **CTRL + A** which will highlight the single space.

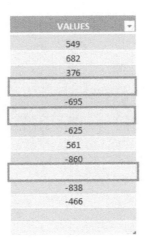

VALUES
549
682
376
-695
-625
561
-860
-838
-466

STEP 1: Go to *Developer > Code > Visual Basic*

STEP 2: Paste in your code and **Select Save**. Close the window afterwards.

```
Sub HighlightTheSingleSpaces()

Dim range As range

For Each range In ActiveSheet.UsedRange
'Check if it's a single space, then change the style to be Note
If range.Value = " " Then
range.Style = "Note"
End If
Next range

End Sub
```

STEP 3: Let us test it out!

Open the sheet containing the data. Go to ***Developer > Code > Macros***

Make sure your Macro is selected. Click **Run**.

With just one click, **all of the cells with a single space are now highlighted!**

Highlight Cells with Comments

What does it do?

Highlights all cells with comments

Copy Source Code:

```
Sub HighlightCellsWithComments()
'Select the cells with comments
Selection.SpecialCells(xlCellTypeComments).Select
'Set all the cells' style to the Note style
Selection.Style= "Note"
End Sub
```

Final Result:

Have a lot of comments in your spreadsheet and want to find all of them? Excel Macros can **highlight all cells with comments** for you!

This is our initial set of data, you can see the ones with the red triangle on the right corner are the ones with comments inserted:

VALUES
-325
-214
-245
-874
-204
-3
947
414
934
-73
-154
-532
348
-579

STEP 1: Go to *Developer > Code > Visual Basic*

STEP 2: Paste in your code and **Select Save**. Close the window afterwards.

```
Sub HighlightCellsWithComments()

'Select the cells with comments
Selection.SpecialCells(xlCellTypeComments).Select

'Set all the cells' style to the Note style
Selection.Style = "Note"

End Sub
```

STEP 3: Let us test it out!

Open the sheet containing the data. Go to *Developer > Code > Macros*

Make sure your Macro is selected. Click **Run**.

With just one click, **all of the cells with comments are now highlighted**!

Highlight Custom Text

What does it do?

Highlights any text that you specify

Copy Source Code:

```vba
Sub HighlightCustomText()

'Get the Custom Text
Dim txt As String
txt = InputBox("Enter the Custom Text", "Enter Text")

Dim rng As Range

'Loop through all values in the selection
For Each rng In Selection

'If the value is the same as the custom text, then set the font
color to red
If rng.Value = txt Then
rng.Font.Color = RGB(255, 0, 0)
End If
Next

End Sub
```

Final Result:

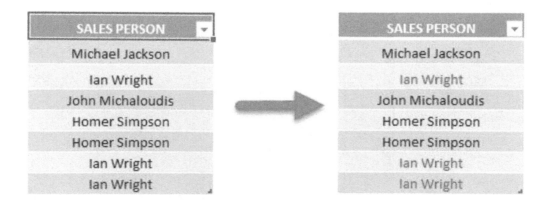

Excel has search text functionality, however we can also use Excel Macros to **highlight custom text**! That's right, you can use it to highlight any text that you specify!

Here is our initial set of data:

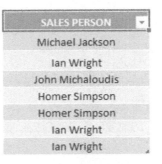

STEP 1: Go to *Developer > Code > Visual Basic*

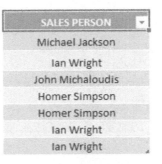

STEP 2: Paste in your code and **Select Save**. Close the window afterwards.

```vba
Sub HighlightCustomText()

'Get the Custom Text
Dim txt As String
txt = InputBox("Enter the Custom Text", "Enter Text")

Dim rng As Range

'Loop through all values in the selection
For Each rng In Selection

'If the value is the same as the custom text, then set the font color to red
If rng.Value = txt Then
rng.Font.Color = RGB(255, 0, 0)
End If
Next

End Sub
```

STEP 3: Let us test it out!

Open the sheet containing the data. Go to *Developer > Code > Macros*

Make sure your Macro is selected. Click **Run**.

For the text, let's type in **Ian Wright**. Click **OK.**

With just one click, **all Ian Wright values are now highlighted**!

Highlight Duplicates

What does it do?

Highlights all cells with duplicate values in a selected range

Copy Source Code:

```
Sub HighlightDuplicates()

Dim cells As Range
Dim cell As Range
Set cells = selection

'Loop through each cell in your selected range looking for
duplicates
For Each cell In cells

'Highlight with a color of your choice, if that cell has
duplicate values
If WorksheetFunction.CountIf(cells, cell.Value) > 1 Then
'Change the ColorIndex into a color you prefer
cell.Interior.ColorIndex = 36
End If
Next cell

End Sub
```

Final Result:

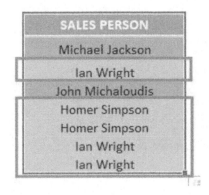

Want to learn how to highlight cells that are duplicates and learn Macros at the same time? Let me show you how to **highlight duplicates using Macros in Excel!**

STEP 1: Go to *Developer > Code > Visual Basic*

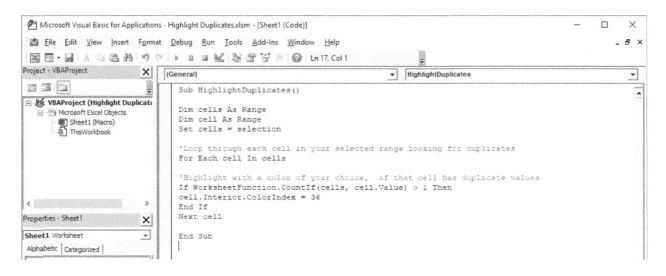

STEP 2: Paste in your code and **Select Save**. Close the window afterwards.

```
Sub HighlightDuplicates()

Dim cells As Range
Dim cell As Range
Set cells = selection

'Loop through each cell in your selected range looking for duplicates
For Each cell In cells

'Highlight with a color of your choice, if that cell has duplicate values
If WorksheetFunction.CountIf(cells, cell.Value) > 1 Then
cell.Interior.ColorIndex = 36
End If
Next cell

End Sub
```

STEP 3: Let us test it out! Make sure to have your cells selected.

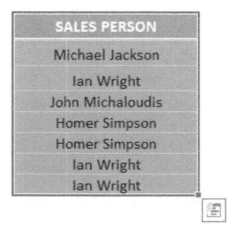

SALES PERSON
Michael Jackson
Ian Wright
John Michaloudis
Homer Simpson
Homer Simpson
Ian Wright
Ian Wright

Open the sheet containing the data. Go to **Developer > Code > Macros**

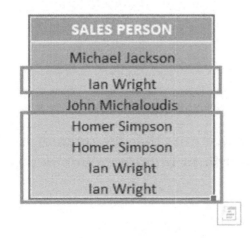

Make sure your Macro is selected. Click **Run**.

With just one click, **all of the duplicate cells now have been highlighted**!

SALES PERSON
Michael Jackson
Ian Wright
John Michaloudis
Homer Simpson
Homer Simpson
Ian Wright
Ian Wright

Highlight Unique Values in Selection

What does it do?

Highlights distinct values in your selection

Copy Source Code:

```
Sub HighlightUniqueValuesInSelection()
'Set the range as the current selection
Dim range As Range
Set range = Selection
range.FormatConditions.Delete
'Color the unique values with green
Dim uniqueVals As UniqueValues
Set uniqueVals = range.FormatConditions.AddUniqueValues
uniqueVals.DupeUnique = xlUnique
uniqueVals.Interior.Color = RGB(0, 255, 0)
End Sub
```

Final Result:

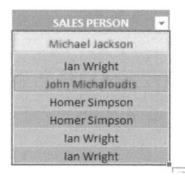

Want to find the values in your list that are unique? It is very easy to do with Excel Macros, you can **highlight unique values** in your selected range in a click!

Here is our initial set of data:

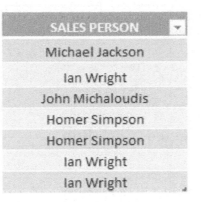

STEP 1: Go to *Developer > Code > Visual Basic*

STEP 2: Paste in your code and **Select Save**. Close the window afterwards.

```
Sub HighlightUniqueValuesInSelection()

'Set the range as the current selection
Dim range As range
Set range = Selection
range.FormatConditions.Delete

'Color the unique values with green
Dim uniqueVals As UniqueValues
Set uniqueVals = range.FormatConditions.AddUniqueValues
uniqueVals.DupeUnique = xlUnique
uniqueVals.Interior.Color = RGB(0, 255, 0)

End Sub
```

STEP 3: Let us test it out!

Open the sheet containing the data. Make sure your data is highlighted. Go to *Developer > Code > Macros*

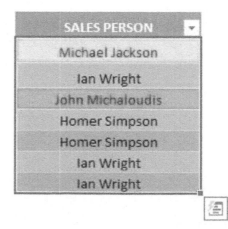

Make sure your Macro is selected. Click **Run**.

With just one click, **all of the unique values are now highlighted**!

Highlight Max Value in Selection

What does it do?

Highlights the largest value in your selection

Copy Source Code:

```vba
Sub HighlightMaxValue()

Dim cell As Range
For Each cell In Selection

'If it matches the highest value, then change the style to be
Note
If cell = WorksheetFunction.Max(Selection) Then
cell.Style = "Note"
End If
Next cell

End Sub
```

Final Result:

VALUES
549
682
376
-774
-695
-264
-625
561
-860
-74
-838
-466
815
227

Have a lot of values and want to find the largest value easily? Excel Macro will do the heavy lifting for you by **highlighting the max value in your selection of values**!

This is our initial set of data:

VALUES
549
682
376
-774
-695
-264
-625
561
-860
-74
-838
-466
815
227

STEP 1: Go to *Developer > Code > Visual Basic*

STEP 2: Paste in your code and **Select Save**. Close the window afterwards.

```
Sub HighlightMaxValue()

Dim cell As Range
For Each cell In Selection

'If it matches the highest value, then change the style to be Note
If cell = WorksheetFunction.Max(Selection) Then
cell.Style = "Note"
End If
Next cell

End Sub
```

STEP 3: Let us test it out! Open the sheet containing the data. Make sure your data is highlighted. Go to *Developer > Code > Macros*

Make sure your Macro is selected. Click **Run**.

With just one click, **your cell with the largest value is now highlighted**!

Highlight Min Value in Selection

What does it do?

Highlights the smallest value in your selection

Copy Source Code:

```
Sub HighlightMinValue()
Dim cell As Range
For Each cell In Selection
'If it matches the smallest value, then change the style to be
Note
If cell = WorksheetFunction.Min(Selection) Then
cell.Style = "Note"
End If
Next cell
End Sub
```

Final Result:

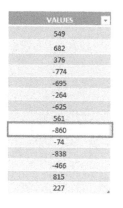

Wanted to find the minimum value in a range of values? Excel Macros can easily **highlight the min value in your selection** for you!

These are our set of values, let us go find the smallest one!

VALUES
549
682
376
-774
-695
-264
-625
561
-860
-74
-838
-466
815
227

STEP 1: Go to *Developer > Code > Visual Basic*

STEP 2: Paste in your code and **Select Save**. Close the window afterwards.

```vba
Sub HighlightMinValue()

Dim cell As Range
For Each cell In Selection

'If it matches the smallest value, then change the style to be Note
If cell = WorksheetFunction.Min(Selection) Then
cell.Style = "Note"
End If
Next cell

End Sub
```

STEP 3: Let us test it out!

Open the sheet containing the data. Make sure your data is highlighted. Go to *Developer > Code > Macros*

Make sure your Macro is selected. Click **Run**.

With just one click, **your cell with the smallest value is now highlighted**!

Highlight Negative Values

What does it do?

Highlights negative values in your selected range

Copy Source Code:

```
Sub HighlightNegativeValues()

Dim NumberToCheck As Range

'Loop through all numbers in the selection
For Each NumberToCheck In Selection
If WorksheetFunction.IsNumber(NumberToCheck) Then
'If it's lesser than 0, then set the font color to red
If NumberToCheck.Value < 0 Then
NumberToCheck.Font.Color= RGB(255, 0, 0)
End If
End If
Next

End Sub
```

Final Result:

VALUES ▼
739
169
-533
-519
-158
-351
580
451
818
-127
-837
344
-678
-693

VALUES ▼
931
649
-602
-350
-208
-953
-819
806
-499
956
98
-392
-608
767

Have a bunch of **negative values** that you want to highlight? You can do that easily through **Excel Macros**!

These are our values:

VALUES
739
169
-533
-519
-158
-351
580
451
818
-127
-837
344
-678
-693

STEP 1: Go to *Developer > Code > Visual Basic*

STEP 2: Paste in your code and **Select Save**. Close the window afterwards.

```vba
Sub HighlightNegativeValues()

Dim NumberToCheck As Range

'Loop through all numbers in the selection
For Each NumberToCheck In Selection
If WorksheetFunction.IsNumber(NumberToCheck) Then
'If it's lesser than 0, then set the font color to red
If NumberToCheck.Value < 0 Then
NumberToCheck.Font.Color = RGB(255, 0, 0)
End If
End If
Next

End Sub
```

STEP 3: Let us test it out!

Open the sheet containing the data. Make sure your data is highlighted. Go to **Developer > Code > Macros**

Make sure your Macro is selected. Click **Run**.

With just one click, **all of the negative values are now marked as color** red!

Highlight Top 10 Values of Selection

What does it do?

Highlights the top 10 values of your selection

Copy Source Code:

```vba
Sub HighlightTopTenValues()

Selection.FormatConditions.AddTop10
Selection.FormatConditions(Selection.FormatConditions.Count).Set
FirstPriority
With Selection.FormatConditions(1)
.TopBottom = xlTop10Top
.Rank = 10
.Percent = False
End With

'Set the font color to red
With Selection.FormatConditions(1).Font
.ColorIndex = 3
.TintAndShade = 0
End With

'Set the highlight color to yellow
With Selection.FormatConditions(1).Interior
.PatternColorIndex = xlAutomatic
.ColorIndex = 27
.TintAndShade = 0
End With

Selection.FormatConditions(1).StopIfTrue = False
End Sub
```

Final Result:

SALES
24,640
24,640
29,923
66,901
63,116
38,281
57,650
90,967
11,910
59,531
88,297
87,868
95,527
90,599
17,030
65,026
57,579
34,338
90,387
62.324

Want to learn how to **highlight the top 10 values** using Macros? We have just the code for you! This one uses Format Conditions to the fullest to achieve this highlighting for you.

STEP 1: Go to *Developer > Code > Visual Basic*

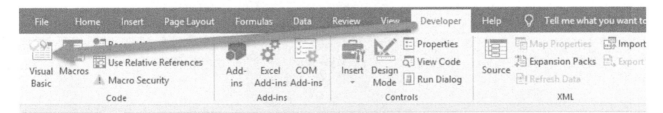

STEP 2: Paste in your code and **Select Save**. Close the window afterwards.

```
Sub HighlightTopTenValues()

Selection.FormatConditions.AddTop10
Selection.FormatConditions(Selection.FormatConditions.Count).SetFirstPriority
With Selection.FormatConditions(1)
.TopBottom = xlTop10Top
.Rank = 10
.Percent = False
End With

'Set the font color to red
With Selection.FormatConditions(1).Font
.ColorIndex = 3
.TintAndShade = 0
End With

'Set the highlight color to yellow
With Selection.FormatConditions(1).Interior
.PatternColorIndex = xlAutomatic
.ColorIndex = 27
.TintAndShade = 0
End With

Selection.FormatConditions(1).StopIfTrue = False
End Sub
```

STEP 3: Let us test it out! Select the data that you want its top 10 values to be highlighted.

SALES
24,640
24,640
29,923
66,901
63,116
38,281
57,650
90,967
11,910
59,531
88,297
87,868
95,527
90,599
17,030
65,026
57,579
34,338
90,387
62,324

Go to *Developer* > *Code* > *Macros*

Make sure your Macro is selected. Click **Run**.

With just one click, **your top 10 values are now highlighted**!

SALES
24,640
24,640
29,923
66,901
63,116
38,281
57,650
90,967
11,910
59,531
88,297
87,868
95,527
90,599
17,030
65,026
57,579
34,338
90,387
62,324

Highlight Bottom 10 Values of Selection

What does it do?

Highlights the bottom 10 values of your selection

Copy Source Code:

```vba
Sub HighlightBottomTenValues()

Selection.FormatConditions.AddTop10
Selection.FormatConditions(Selection.FormatConditions.Count).Set
FirstPriority
With Selection.FormatConditions(1)
.TopBottom = xlTop10Bottom
.Rank = 10
.Percent = False
End With

'Set the font color to red
With Selection.FormatConditions(1).Font
.ColorIndex = 3
.TintAndShade = 0
End With

'Set the highlight color to yellow
With Selection.FormatConditions(1).Interior
.PatternColorIndex = xlAutomatic
.ColorIndex = 27
.TintAndShade = 0
End With

Selection.FormatConditions(1).StopIfTrue = False
End Sub
```

Final Result:

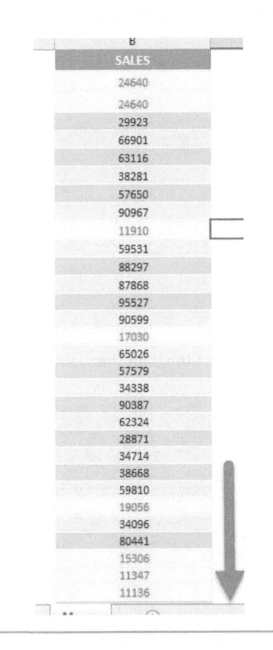

Want to learn how to **highlight the bottom 10 values** using Macros? We have just the code for you! This one uses Format Conditions to the fullest to achieve this highlighting for you.

STEP 1: Go to *Developer > Code > Visual Basic*

STEP 2: Paste in your code and **Select Save**. Close the window afterwards.

```vba
Sub HighlightBottomTenValues()

Selection.FormatConditions.AddTop10
Selection.FormatConditions(Selection.FormatConditions.Count).SetFirstPriority
With Selection.FormatConditions(1)
.TopBottom = xlTop10Bottom
.Rank = 10
.Percent = False
End With

'Set the font color to red
With Selection.FormatConditions(1).Font
.ColorIndex = 3
.TintAndShade = 0
End With

'Set the highlight color to yellow
With Selection.FormatConditions(1).Interior
.PatternColorIndex = xlAutomatic
.ColorIndex = 27
.TintAndShade = 0
End With

Selection.FormatConditions(1).StopIfTrue = False
End Sub
```

STEP 3: Let us test it out! Select the data that you want its bottom 10 values to be highlighted.

SALES
24,640
24,640
29,923
66,901
63,116
38,281
57,650
90,967
11,910
59,531
88,297
87,868
95,527
90,599
17,030
65,026
57,579
34,338
90,387
62,324

Go to *Developer > Code > Macros*

Make sure your Macro is selected. Click **Run**.

With just one click, **your bottom 10 values are now highlighted**!

Highlight Values Greater Than

What does it do?

Highlights values greater than your specified value

Copy Source Code:

```
Sub HighlightValuesGreaterThan()

'Get the Greater Than Value
Dim value As Long
value = InputBox("Enter Greater Than Value", "Enter Greater Than
Value")

Selection.FormatConditions.Delete
Selection.FormatConditions.Add Type:=xlCellValue,
Operator:=xlGreater, Formula1:=value
Selection.FormatConditions(Selection.FormatConditions.Count).Set
FirstPriority

'Set the font to black and highlighting color as yellow
With Selection.FormatConditions(1)
.Font.Color = RGB(0, 0, 0)
.Interior.Color = RGB(255, 255, 0)
End With

End Sub
```

Final Result:

SALES
24640
24640
29923
66901
63116
38281
57650
90967
11910
59531
88297
87868
95527
90599

You will be surprised on how much you can do with Macros. It can **highlight values** in your selected range that are **greater than a value you specify.**

These are our values:

SALES
24640
24640
29923
66901
63116
38281
57650
90967
11910
59531
88297
87868
95527
90599

STEP 1: Go to *Developer > Code > Visual Basic*

STEP 2: Paste in your code and **Select Save**. Close the window afterwards.

```
Sub HighlightValuesGreaterThan()

'Get the Greater Than Value
Dim value As Long
value = InputBox("Enter Greater Than Value", "Enter Greater Than Value")

Selection.FormatConditions.Delete
Selection.FormatConditions.Add Type:=xlCellValue, Operator:=xlGreater, Formula1:=value
Selection.FormatConditions(Selection.FormatConditions.Count).SetFirstPriority

'Set the font to black and highlighting color as yellow
With Selection.FormatConditions(1)
.Font.Color = RGB(0, 0, 0)
.Interior.Color = RGB(255, 255, 0)
End With

End Sub
```

STEP 3: Let us test it out!

Open the sheet containing the data. Make sure your data is highlighted. Go to *Developer > Code > Macros*

Make sure your Macro is selected. Click **Run**.

Enter the greater than value, we will enter 50000. Click **OK**.

SALES	▼
24640	
24640	
29923	
66901	
63116	
38281	
57650	
90967	
11910	
59531	
88297	
87868	
95527	
90599	

Enter Greater Than Value   ✕

Enter Greater Than Value

> [OK]
> [Cancel]

50000

With just one click, **all of the values greater than 50,000 are now highlighted**!

SALES	▼
24640	
24640	
29923	
66901	
63116	
38281	
57650	
90967	
11910	
59531	
88297	
87868	
95527	
90599	

Highlight Values Lesser Than

What does it do?

Highlights values lesser than your specified value

Copy Source Code:

```vba
Sub HighlightValuesLesserThan()

'Get the Lesser Than Value
Dim value As Long
value = InputBox("Enter Lesser Than Value", "Enter Lesser Than
Value")

Selection.FormatConditions.Delete
Selection.FormatConditions.Add Type:=xlCellValue,
Operator:=xlLess, Formula1:=value
Selection.FormatConditions(Selection.FormatConditions.Count).Set
FirstPriority

'Set the font to black and highlighting color as yellow
With Selection.FormatConditions(1)
.Font.Color = RGB(0, 0, 0)
.Interior.Color = RGB(255,255, 0)
End With
End Sub
```

Final Result:

SALES
24640
24640
29923
66901
63116
38281
57650
90967
11910
59531
88297
87868
95527
90599

Want to try something new with Macros? You can **highlight values** in your selected range that are **lesser than a value you specify**.

These are our values:

SALES
24640
24640
29923
66901
63116
38281
57650
90967
11910
59531
88297
87868
95527
90599

STEP 1: Go to *Developer > Code > Visual Basic*

STEP 2: Paste in your code and **Select Save**. Close the window afterwards.

```
Sub HighlightValuesLesserThan()

'Get the Lesser Than Value
Dim value As Long
value = InputBox("Enter Lesser Than Value", "Enter Lesser Than Value")

Selection.FormatConditions.Delete
Selection.FormatConditions.Add Type:=xlCellValue, Operator:=xlLess, Formula1:=value
Selection.FormatConditions(Selection.FormatConditions.Count).SetFirstPriority

'Set the font to black and highlighting color as yellow
With Selection.FormatConditions(1)
.Font.Color = RGB(0, 0, 0)
.Interior.Color = RGB(255, 255, 0)
End With
End Sub
```

STEP 3: Let us test it out!

Open the sheet containing the data. Make sure your data is highlighted. Go to **Developer > Code > Macros**

Make sure your Macro is selected. Click **Run**.

Enter the lesser than value, we will enter 50000. Click **OK**.

SALES	
24640	
24640	
29923	
66901	
63116	
38281	
57650	
90967	
11910	
59531	
88297	
87868	
95527	
90599	

Enter Lesser Than Value

Enter Lesser Than Value

OK

Cancel

50000

With just one click, **all of the values lesser than 50,000 are now highlighted**!

SALES	
24640	
24640	
29923	
66901	
63116	
38281	
57650	
90967	
11910	
59531	
88297	
87868	
95527	
90599	

Spell check and Highlight Misspellings

What does it do?

Highlights the cells with incorrect spelling

Copy Source Code:

```
Sub HighlightMisspellings()
Dim cell As range
For Each cell In ActiveSheet.UsedRange
'Check the spelling and if it's wrong, then change the style to
be Bad
If Not Application.CheckSpelling(word:=cell.Text) Then
cell.Style = "Bad"
End If
Next cell
End Sub
```

Final Result:

VALUES
Hello World
Thank You
How's thier dog?
How's their dog?
What is your adress?
My spelling is top nothc.
This is cool!

Excel has spell checking functionality, and we can take this to the next level by using Excel Macros to spell check then **highlight misspellings** for you!

STEP 1: Go to *Developer > Code > Visual Basic*

STEP 2: Paste in your code and **Select Save**. Close the window afterwards.

```vba
Sub HighlightMisspellings()

Dim cell As range
For Each cell In ActiveSheet.UsedRange

'Check the spelling and if it's wrong, then change the style to be Bad
If Not Application.CheckSpelling(word:=cell.Text) Then
cell.Style = "Bad"
End If

Next cell

End Sub
```

STEP 3: Let us test it out!

Open the sheet containing the data. Go to *Developer > Code > Macros*

Make sure your Macro is selected. Click **Run**.

ell check and
ng Macros in

Macro ? ✕

Macro name:

Sheet1.HighlightMisspellings ⬆

Sheet1.HighlightMisspellings

VALUES
Hello World
Thank You
How's thier dog?
How's their dog?
What is your adress?
My spelling is top nothc.
This is cool!

Macros in: All Open Workbooks

Description

Run

Step Into

Edit

Create

Delete

Options...

Cancel

lacro ⊕

With just one click, **all of the cells with incorrect spellings are now highlighted**!

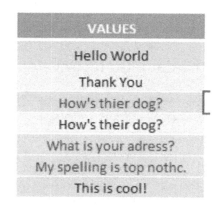

VALUES
Hello World
Thank You
How's thier dog?
How's their dog?
What is your adress?
My spelling is top nothc.
This is cool!

PIVOT TABLE MACROS

Disable Enable Get Pivot Data

What does it do?

Disable / Enable Get Pivot Data

Copy Source Code:

```
Sub EnableGetPivotData()
Application.GenerateGetPivotData = True
End Sub

Sub DisableGetPivotData()
Application.GenerateGetPivotData = False
End Sub
```

Final Result:

Row Labels	Sum of SALES	
2014	7000000	=GETPIVOTDATA("SALES",A7,"YEAR",2014)
EAST	2000000	
NORTH	1000000	
SOUTH	1500000	
WEST	2500000	
2015	250014	
EAST	57650	
NORTH	63116	
SOUTH	38281	
WEST	90967	
Grand Total	7250014	

Row Labels	Sum of SALES	
2014	7000000	=B8
EAST	2000000	
NORTH	1000000	
SOUTH	1500000	
WEST	2500000	
2015	250014	
EAST	57650	
NORTH	63116	
SOUTH	38281	
WEST	90967	
Grand Total	7250014	

When you wanted to reference a cell in a Pivot Table, a GETPIVOTDATA formula shows up instead. If you want to have just a normal cell reference show up, you can **disable/enable get pivot data** using Excel Macros!

Row Labels	Sum of SALES	
2014	7000000	=GETPIVOTDATA("SALES",A7,"YEAR",2014)
EAST	2000000	
NORTH	1000000	
SOUTH	1500000	
WEST	2500000	
2015	250014	
EAST	57650	
NORTH	63116	
SOUTH	38281	
WEST	90967	
Grand Total	7250014	

Here is our pivot table:

Row Labels ▾	Sum of SALES
⊟ 2014	7000000
EAST	2000000
NORTH	1000000
SOUTH	1500000
WEST	2500000
⊟ 2015	250014
EAST	57650
NORTH	63116
SOUTH	38281
WEST	90967
Grand Total	7250014

If we try to create a formula involving one of the cells inside the Pivot Table, you will see the **GETPIVOTDATA Formula**. Let us change this behavior using Macros!

Row Labels ▾	Sum of SALES	
⊟ 2014	7000000	=GETPIVOTDATA("SALES",A7,"YEAR",2014)
EAST	2000000	
NORTH	1000000	
SOUTH	1500000	
WEST	2500000	
⊟ 2015	250014	
EAST	57650	
NORTH	63116	
SOUTH	38281	
WEST	90967	
Grand Total	7250014	

STEP 1: Go to *Developer > Code > Visual Basic*

STEP 2: Paste in your code and **Select Save**. This will create two options for you to choose either to enable or disable. Close the window afterwards.

```
Sub EnableGetPivotData()
Application.GenerateGetPivotData = True
End Sub

Sub DisableGetPivotData()
Application.GenerateGetPivotData = False
End Sub
```

STEP 3: Let us test it out!

Open the sheet containing the data. Go to *Developer > Code > Macros*

Make sure your disable Macro is selected. Click **Run**.

Row Labels ⏷	Sum of SALES
⊟ 2014	**7000000**
EAST	2000000
NORTH	1000000
SOUTH	1500000
WEST	2500000
⊟ 2015	**250014**
EAST	57650
NORTH	63116
SOUTH	38281
WEST	90967
Grand Total	**7250014**

Macro ? ✕

Macro name:

Sheet1.DisableGetPivotData

> Sheet1.DisableGetPivotData
> Sheet1.EnableGetPivotData

Run

Step Into

Edit

Create

Delete

Options...

Macros in: All Open Workbooks

Description

Try referencing a cell inside the pivot table again. It is now a normal cell reference.

With just one click, **we have disabled get pivot data**!

Row Labels ⏷	Sum of SALES	
⊟ **2014**	**7000000**	=B8
EAST	2000000	
NORTH	1000000	
SOUTH	1500000	
WEST	2500000	
⊟ **2015**	**250014**	
EAST	57650	
NORTH	63116	
SOUTH	38281	
WEST	90967	
Grand Total	**7250014**	

Hide Pivot Table Subtotals

What does it do?

Hide the Pivot Table subtotals

Copy Source Code:

```vba
'Select a cell first from your pivot table
Sub HidePivotTableSubtotals()

Dim pTable As PivotTable
Dim pField As PivotField

On Error Resume Next

'Get the pivot table first
Set pTable = ActiveSheet.PivotTables(ActiveCell.PivotTable.name)

'Check if a pivot table is found
If pTable Is Nothing Then
MsgBox "Please select a cell first from your Pivot Table."
Exit Sub
End If

'For each subtotal, make it hidden
For Each pField In pTable.PivotFields
pField.Subtotals(1) = True
pField.Subtotals(1) = False
Next pField

End Sub
```

Final Result:

Row Labels	Sum of SALES			Row Labels	Sum of SALES
2014				2014	
EAST	2000000			EAST	2000000
NORTH	1000000			NORTH	1000000
SOUTH	1500000			SOUTH	1500000
WEST	2500000	→		WEST	2500000
2014 Total	7000000			2015	
2015				EAST	57650
EAST	57650			NORTH	63116
NORTH	63116			SOUTH	38281
SOUTH	38281			WEST	90967
WEST	90967			Grand Total	7250014
2015 Total	250014				
Grand Total	7250014				

Excel Macros encompass a lot of functionality, and modifying Pivot Tables is one of them! Let us **hide pivot table subtotals** using Excel Macros!

This is our Pivot Table and we want to hide these subtotals:

Row Labels	Sum of SALES
2014	
EAST	2000000
NORTH	1000000
SOUTH	1500000
WEST	2500000
2014 Total	7000000
2015	
EAST	57650
NORTH	63116
SOUTH	38281
WEST	90967
2015 Total	250014
Grand Total	7250014

STEP 1: Go to *Developer* > *Code* > *Visual Basic*

STEP 2: Paste in your code and **Select Save**. Close the window afterwards.

```
On Error Resume Next

'Get the pivot table first
Set pTable = ActiveSheet.PivotTables(ActiveCell.PivotTable.Name)

'Check if a pivot table is found
If pTable Is Nothing Then
MsgBox "Please select a cell first from your Pivot Table."
Exit Sub
End If

'For each subtotal, make it hidden
For Each pField In pTable.PivotFields
pField.Subtotals(1) = True
pField.Subtotals(1) = False
Next pField

End Sub
```

STEP 3: Let us test it out!

Open the sheet containing the data. Make sure your pivot table is selected. Go to *Developer* > *Code* > *Macros*

Make sure your Macro is selected. Click **Run**.

Row Labels ▾	Sum of SALES
⊟ 2014	
EAST	2000000
NORTH	1000000
SOUTH	1500000
WEST	2500000
2014 Total	**7000000**
⊟ 2015	
EAST	57650
NORTH	63116
SOUTH	38281
WEST	90967
2015 Total	**250014**
Grand Total	**7250014**

Macro ? ✕

Macro name:

Sheet1.HidePivotTableSubtotals	⬆		Run
Sheet1.HidePivotTableSubtotals	⌃		Step Into
			Edit
			Create
			Delete
	⌄		Options...

Macros in: All Open Workbooks ⌄

Description

Cancel

With just one click, **your Pivot Table subtotals are now hidden**!

Row Labels ▾	Sum of SALES
⊟ 2014	
EAST	2000000
NORTH	1000000
SOUTH	1500000
WEST	2500000
⊟ 2015	
EAST	57650
NORTH	63116
SOUTH	38281
WEST	90967
Grand Total	**7250014**

Refresh All Pivot Tables

What does it do?

Refresh all Pivot Tables

Copy Source Code:

```
Sub RefreshAllPivotTables()

Dim pCache As PivotCache

'With just one loop, refresh all pivot tables!
For Each pCache In ActiveWorkbook.PivotCaches
pCache.Refresh
Next pCache

End Sub
```

Final Result:

Row Labels ▾	Sum of SALES
Homer Simpson	8336813
Ian Wright	8071721
John Michaloudis	8158034
Michael Jackson	7497764
Grand Total	32064332

Row Labels ▾	Sum of SALES
AFRICA	8336813
AMERICAS	7497764
ASIA	8158034
EUROPE	8071721
Grand Total	32064332

Row Labels ▾	Sum of SALES
Homer Simpson	8336813
Ian Wright	8071721
John Michaloudis	8158034
Michael Jackson	130929913
Grand Total	155496481

Row Labels ▾	Sum of SALES
AFRICA	8336813
AMERICAS	130929913
ASIA	8158034
EUROPE	8071721
Grand Total	155496481

It is so frequent that whenever I update my data, I forget to refresh my Pivot Tables. We can now **refresh all pivot tables** using Excel Macros!

This is our data:

	CUSTOMER	PRODUCTS	SALES PERSON	SALES REGION	ORDER DATE	SALES	FINANCIAL YEAR	SALES MONTH	SALES QTR	CHANNEL PARTNERS
2	LONG ISLANDS INC	SOFT DRINKS	Michael Jackson	AMERICAS	13/04/2012	24,640	2012	January	Q1	Acme, inc.
3	LONG ISLANDS INC	SOFT DRINKS	Michael Jackson	AMERICAS	21/12/2012	24,640	2012	February	Q1	Widget Corp
4	LONG ISLANDS INC	SOFT DRINKS	Michael Jackson	AMERICAS	24/12/2012	29,923	2012	March	Q1	123 Warehousing
5	LONG ISLANDS INC	SOFT DRINKS	Michael Jackson	AMERICAS	24/12/2012	66,901	2012	April	Q2	Demo Company
6	LONG ISLANDS INC	SOFT DRINKS	Michael Jackson	AMERICAS	29/12/2012	63,116	2012	May	Q2	Smith and Co.
7	LONG ISLANDS INC	SOFT DRINKS	Michael Jackson	AMERICAS	28/06/2012	38,281	2012	June	Q2	Foo Bars
8	LONG ISLANDS INC	SOFT DRINKS	Michael Jackson	AMERICAS	28/06/2012	57,650	2012	July	Q3	ABC Telecom
9	LONG ISLANDS INC	SOFT DRINKS	Michael Jackson	AMERICAS	29/06/2012	11,910	2012	August	Q3	Fake Brothers
10	LONG ISLANDS INC	SOFT DRINKS	Michael Jackson	AMERICAS	29/06/2012	90,967	2012	September	Q3	QWERTY Logistics
11	LONG ISLANDS INC	SOFT DRINKS	Michael Jackson	AMERICAS	06/07/2012	59,531	2012	October	Q4	Demo, inc.
12	LONG ISLANDS INC	SOFT DRINKS	Michael Jackson	AMERICAS	06/07/2012	88,297	2012	November	Q4	Sample Company
13	LONG ISLANDS INC	SOFT DRINKS	Michael Jackson	AMERICAS	08/09/2012	87,868	2012	December	Q4	Sample, inc
14	LONG ISLANDS INC	BOTTLES	Michael Jackson	AMERICAS	08/09/2012	95,527	2012	January	Q1	Acme Corp
15	LONG ISLANDS INC	BOTTLES	Michael Jackson	AMERICAS	30/06/2012	90,599	2012	February	Q1	Allied Biscuit

These are the two pivot tables using this data source:

Row Labels	▾	Sum of SALES
Homer Simpson		8336813
Ian Wright		8071721
John Michaloudis		8158034
Michael Jackson		7497764
Grand Total		**32064332**

Row Labels	▾	Sum of SALES
AFRICA		8336813
AMERICAS		7497764
ASIA		8158034
EUROPE		8071721
Grand Total		**32064332**

Now let's make change to have one big sales value! Let us see if the pivot tables will reflect these values.

	A	B	C	D	E	F	G	H	I	J
1	CUSTOMER	PRODUCTS	SALES PERSON	SALES REGION	ORDER DATE	SALES	FINANCIAL YEAR	SALES MONTH	SALES QTR	CHANNEL PARTNERS
2	LONG ISLANDS INC	SOFT DRINKS	Michael Jackson	AMERICAS	13/04/2012	123,456,789	2012	January	Q1	Acme, inc.
3	LONG ISLANDS INC	SOFT DRINKS	Michael Jackson	AMERICAS	21/12/2012	24,640	2012	February	Q1	Widget Corp
4	LONG ISLANDS INC	SOFT DRINKS	Michael Jackson	AMERICAS	24/12/2012	29,923	2012	March	Q1	123 Warehousing
5	LONG ISLANDS INC	SOFT DRINKS	Michael Jackson	AMERICAS	24/12/2012	66,901	2012	April	Q2	Demo Company

STEP 1: Go to *Developer > Code > Visual Basic*

STEP 2: Paste in your code and **Select Save**. Close the window afterwards.

```
Sub RefreshAllPivotTables()

Dim pCache As PivotCache

'With just one loop, refresh all pivot tables!
For Each pCache In ActiveWorkbook.PivotCaches
pCache.Refresh
Next pCache

End Sub
```

STEP 3: Let us test it out!

Open the sheet containing the data. Go to *Developer > Code > Macros*

Make sure your Macro is selected. Click **Run**.

With just one click, **all of your pivot tables are now refreshed**!

Row Labels	Sum of SALES
Homer Simpson	8336813
Ian Wright	8071721
John Michaloudis	8158034
Michael Jackson	130929913
Grand Total	155496481

Row Labels	Sum of SALES
AFRICA	8336813
AMERICAS	130929913
ASIA	8158034
EUROPE	8071721
Grand Total	155496481

Remove Autofit Columns on Refresh

What does it do?

Removes the Autofit Columns setting of all Pivot Tables whenever you refresh the Pivot Tables

Copy Source Code:

```
Sub RemoveAutofitColumnsOnRefresh()

Dim pvtTable As PivotTable

For Each pvtTable In ActiveSheet.PivotTables
  pvtTable.HasAutoFormat = False
Next pvtTable

End Sub
```

Final Result:

It is so frequent that whenever I update my data, I lose the formatting of my Pivot Table column widths and they become autofitted.

We can now **remove the autofit columns setting of all pivot tables** using Excel Macros!

This is our data:

To demonstrate, let us try to refresh all pivot tables and see if the columns get autofitted. Go to **Data > Connections > Refresh All**

You can see our columns got autofitted (Column E stands out). Let us turn this off with Excel Macros! Now press **the undo button** to undo the change we made.

STEP 1: Go to *Developer* > *Code* > *Visual Basic*

STEP 2: Paste in your code and **Select Save**. Close the window afterwards.

```
Sub RemoveAutofitColumnsOnRefresh()

Dim pvtTable As PivotTable

For Each pvtTable In ActiveSheet.PivotTables
  pvtTable.HasAutoFormat = False
Next pvtTable

End Sub
```

STEP 3: Let us test it out!

Open the sheet containing the data. Go to *Developer* > *Code* > *Macros*

Make sure your Macro is selected. Click **Run**.

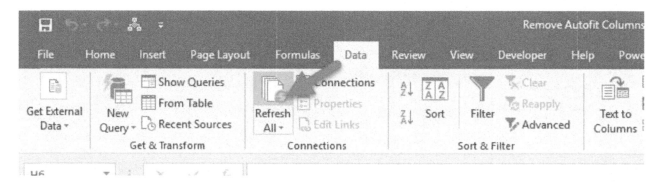

Now let us refresh all the pivot tables. Go to **Data > Connections > Refresh All**

All of your pivot tables are now refreshed and **have kept their original column widths**!

	A	B	C	D	E	F
1						
2						
3						
4						
5						
6	**Row Labels**	**Sum of SALES**		**Row Labels**	**Sum of SALES**	
7	Homer Simpson	8336813		AFRICA	8336813	
8	Ian Wright	8071721		AMERICAS	19818802	
9	John Michaloudis	8158034		ASIA	8158034	
10	Michael Jackson	19818802		EUROPE	8071721	
11	**Grand Total**	**44385370**		**Grand Total**	**44385370**	

PRINTING MACROS

Print All Comments of a Worksheet

What does it do?

Prints all comments of a specific worksheet to the last page

Copy Source Code:

```
Sub PrintCommentsToLastPage()
'Print all comments to the last page
With ActiveSheet.PageSetup
.printComments= xlPrintSheetEnd
End With
End Sub
```

Final Result:

Want to quickly collate the comments in your spreadsheet? Excel Macros will do the hard work for you, by **printing all comments of a worksheet to the last page**!

We've added a couple of comments to these cells below. Let us see how it will look like!

	A	B	C	D	E	F	G	H	I	J
1	CUSTOMER	PRODUCTS	SALES PERSON	SALES REGION	ORDER DATE	SALES	FINANCIAL YEAR	SALES MONTH	SALES QTR	CHANNEL PARTNERS
2	LONG ISLANDS INC	SOFT DRINKS	Michael Jackson	AMERICAS	13/04/2012	24,640	2012	January	Q1	Acme, inc.
3	LONG ISLANDS INC	SOFT DRINKS	Michael Jackson	AMERICAS	21/12/2012	24,640	2012	February	Q1	Widget Corp
4	LONG ISLANDS INC	SOFT DRINKS	Michael Jackson	AMERICAS	24/12/2012	29,923	2012	March	Q1	123 Warehousing
5	LONG ISLANDS INC	SOFT DRINKS	Michael Jackson	AMERICAS	24/12/2012	66,901	2012	April	Q2	Demo Company
6	LONG ISLANDS INC	SOFT DRINKS	Michael Jackson	AMERICAS	29/12/2012	63.116	2012	May	Q2	Smith and Co.

STEP 1: Go to *Developer > Code > Visual Basic*

STEP 2: Paste in your code and **Select Save**. Close the window afterwards.

STEP 3: Let us test it out!

Open the sheet containing the data. Go to *Developer > Code > Macros*

Make sure your Macro is selected. Click **Run**.

Macro   ?   ✕

Macro name:

Sheet1.PrintCommentsToLastPage   ⬆   [Run]

Sheet1.PrintCommentsToLastPage   [Step Into]

                                                     [Edit]

Go to *File > Print*

Save

Save As

History

Print

Share

Export

Publish

Close

Scroll to the last page. You can now see the following information for the **comments**: Cell location, comment and the author of the comment!

Print All Comments to Last Page.xlsm - Excel   Sign in   ?   —   ⬜   ✕

Print

Copies: 1

Print

Printer
Fax
Ready

Printer Properties

Settings

Print Active Sheets
Only print the active sheets

Pages: to

Collated
1,2,3   1,2,3   1,2,3

Portrait Orientation

Letter
21.59 cm x 27.94 cm

Normal Margins
Left: 1.78 cm   Right: 1.78 cm

No Scaling
Print sheets at their actual size

Page Setup

Cell: A1
Comment: MyExcelOnline:
         Customer who purchased the items

Cell: D1
Comment: MyExcelOnline:
         There are 4 main regions

Cell: F1
Comment: MyExcelOnline:
         Currency is in USD

Cell: J1
Comment: MyExcelOnline:
         Double check the Channel Partner name first in your reports

◀ 3   of 3 ▶

Print the Selected Area

What does it do?

Prints out the selected area

Copy Source Code:

```
Sub PrintTheSelectedArea()

'Print out a copy of your selected area
Selection.PrintOut Copies:=1

End Sub
```

Final Result:

CUSTOMER	PRODUCTS	SALES PERSON	SALES REGION	ORDER DATE	SALES
LONG ISLANDS INC	SOFT DRINKS	Michael Jackson	AMERICAS	13/04/2012	24,640
LONG ISLANDS INC	SOFT DRINKS	Michael Jackson	AMERICAS	21/12/2012	24,640
LONG ISLANDS INC	SOFT DRINKS	Michael Jackson	AMERICAS	24/12/2012	29,923
LONG ISLANDS INC	SOFT DRINKS	Michael Jackson	AMERICAS	24/12/2012	66,901
LONG ISLANDS INC	SOFT DRINKS	Michael Jackson	AMERICAS	29/12/2012	63,116
LONG ISLANDS INC	SOFT DRINKS	Michael Jackson	AMERICAS	28/06/2012	38,281
LONG ISLANDS INC	SOFT DRINKS	Michael Jackson	AMERICAS	28/06/2012	57,650
LONG ISLANDS INC	SOFT DRINKS	Michael Jackson	AMERICAS	29/06/2012	90,967

Did you know that you could print out a specific area in your spreadsheet? Yes that's right, you can use Excel Macro to just print the selected area you have chosen! You get to save some printer ink in the process as well!

STEP 1: Go to *Developer > Code > Visual Basic*

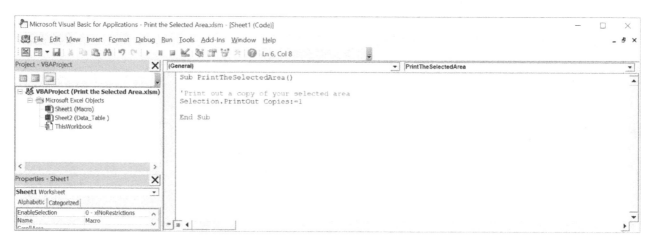

STEP 2: Paste in your code and **Select Save**. Close the window afterwards.

STEP 3: Let us test it out! Select the area that you only want to print.

Open the sheet containing the data. Make sure your data is highlighted. Go to *Developer > Code > Macros*

Make sure your Macro is selected. Click **Run**.

With this, **you have printed out the selected area only**!

CUSTOMER	PRODUCTS	SALES PERSON	SALES REGION	ORDER DATE	SALES
LONG ISLANDS INC	SOFT DRINKS	Michael Jackson	AMERICAS	13/04/2012	24,640
LONG ISLANDS INC	SOFT DRINKS	Michael Jackson	AMERICAS	21/12/2012	24,640
LONG ISLANDS INC	SOFT DRINKS	Michael Jackson	AMERICAS	24/12/2012	29,923
LONG ISLANDS INC	SOFT DRINKS	Michael Jackson	AMERICAS	24/12/2012	66,901
LONG ISLANDS INC	SOFT DRINKS	Michael Jackson	AMERICAS	29/12/2012	63,116
LONG ISLANDS INC	SOFT DRINKS	Michael Jackson	AMERICAS	28/06/2012	38,281
LONG ISLANDS INC	SOFT DRINKS	Michael Jackson	AMERICAS	28/06/2012	57,650
LONG ISLANDS INC	SOFT DRINKS	Michael Jackson	AMERICAS	29/06/2012	90,967

Print with a Narrow Margin

What does it do?

Prints out with narrow margins then shows the print dialog

Copy Source Code:

```vba
Sub PrintWithNarrowMargin()

'Set the Margins to be narrow and print it out
With ActiveSheet.PageSetup
.HeaderMargin= Application.InchesToPoints(0.3)
.FooterMargin= Application.InchesToPoints(0.3)
.LeftMargin= Application.InchesToPoints(0.25)
.RightMargin= Application.InchesToPoints(0.25)
.TopMargin= Application.InchesToPoints(0.75)
.BottomMargin= Application.InchesToPoints(0.75)
End With

Application.Dialogs(xlDialogPrint).Show

End Sub
```

Final Result:

CUSTOMER	PRODUCTS	SALES PERSON	SALES REGION	ORDER DATE	SALES
LONG ISLANDS INC	SOFT DRINKS	Michael Jackson	AMERICAS	13/04/2012	24,640
LONG ISLANDS INC	SOFT DRINKS	Michael Jackson	AMERICAS	21/12/2012	24,640
LONG ISLANDS INC	SOFT DRINKS	Michael Jackson	AMERICAS	24/12/2012	29,923
LONG ISLANDS INC	SOFT DRINKS	Michael Jackson	AMERICAS	24/12/2012	66,901
LONG ISLANDS INC	SOFT DRINKS	Michael Jackson	AMERICAS	29/12/2012	63,116
LONG ISLANDS INC	SOFT DRINKS	Michael Jackson	AMERICAS	28/06/2012	38,281
LONG ISLANDS INC	SOFT DRINKS	Michael Jackson	AMERICAS	28/06/2012	57,650
LONG ISLANDS INC	SOFT DRINKS	Michael Jackson	AMERICAS	29/06/2012	90,967
LONG ISLANDS INC	SOFT DRINKS	Michael Jackson	AMERICAS	29/06/2012	11,910
LONG ISLANDS INC	SOFT DRINKS	Michael Jackson	AMERICAS	06/07/2012	59,531
LONG ISLANDS INC	SOFT DRINKS	Michael Jackson	AMERICAS	06/07/2012	88,297
LONG ISLANDS INC	SOFT DRINKS	Michael Jackson	AMERICAS	08/09/2012	87,868
LONG ISLANDS INC	BOTTLES	Michael Jackson	AMERICAS	08/09/2012	95,527
LONG ISLANDS INC	BOTTLES	Michael Jackson	AMERICAS	30/06/2012	90,599
LONG ISLANDS INC	BOTTLES	Michael Jackson	AMERICAS	23/12/2012	17,030
LONG ISLANDS INC	BOTTLES	Michael Jackson	AMERICAS	08/12/2012	65,026
LONG ISLANDS INC	BOTTLES	Michael Jackson	AMERICAS	28/10/2012	57,579
LONG ISLANDS INC	BOTTLES	Michael Jackson	AMERICAS	28/10/2012	34,338
LONG ISLANDS INC	BOTTLES	Michael Jackson	AMERICAS	15/09/2012	90,387
LONG ISLANDS INC	BOTTLES	Michael Jackson	AMERICAS	28/10/2012	62,324
LONG ISLANDS INC	BOTTLES	Michael Jackson	AMERICAS	31/10/2012	28,871
LONG ISLANDS INC	BOTTLES	Michael Jackson	AMERICAS	29/12/2012	34,714

In Excel we can opt to print out with very narrow margins through its interface. We can do the same thing with Excel Macros, you can **print with a narrow margin**, or even customize the margin values so that it will be constant every time!

This is our data table:

	CUSTOMER	PRODUCTS	SALES PERSON	SALES REGION	ORDER DATE	SALES	FINANCIAL YEAR	SALES MONTH	SALES QTR	CHANNEL PARTNERS
2	LONG ISLANDS INC	SOFT DRINKS	Michael Jackson	AMERICAS	13/04/2012	24,640	2012	January	Q1	Acme, inc.
3	LONG ISLANDS INC	SOFT DRINKS	Michael Jackson	AMERICAS	21/12/2012	24,640	2012	February	Q1	Widget Corp
4	LONG ISLANDS INC	SOFT DRINKS	Michael Jackson	AMERICAS	24/12/2012	29,023	2012	March	Q1	123 Warehousing
5	LONG ISLANDS INC	SOFT DRINKS	Michael Jackson	AMERICAS	24/12/2012	66,901	2012	April	Q2	Demo Company
6	LONG ISLANDS INC	SOFT DRINKS	Michael Jackson	AMERICAS	29/12/2012	63,116	2012	May	Q2	Smith and Co.
7	LONG ISLANDS INC	SOFT DRINKS	Michael Jackson	AMERICAS	28/06/2012	38,281	2012	June	Q2	Foo Bars
8	LONG ISLANDS INC	SOFT DRINKS	Michael Jackson	AMERICAS	28/06/2012	57,650	2012	July	Q3	ABC Telecom
9	LONG ISLANDS INC	SOFT DRINKS	Michael Jackson	AMERICAS	29/06/2012	90,967	2012	August	Q3	Fake Brothers
10	LONG ISLANDS INC	SOFT DRINKS	Michael Jackson	AMERICAS	29/06/2012	11,910	2012	September	Q3	QWERTY Logistics
11	LONG ISLANDS INC	SOFT DRINKS	Michael Jackson	AMERICAS	06/07/2012	59,531	2012	October	Q4	Demo, inc.
12	LONG ISLANDS INC	SOFT DRINKS	Michael Jackson	AMERICAS	06/07/2012	88,297	2012	November	Q4	Sample Company
13	LONG ISLANDS INC	SOFT DRINKS	Michael Jackson	AMERICAS	08/09/2012	87,868	2012	December	Q4	Sample, inc
14	LONG ISLANDS INC	BOTTLES	Michael Jackson	AMERICAS	08/09/2012	95,527	2012	January	Q1	Acme Corp
15	LONG ISLANDS INC	BOTTLES	Michael Jackson	AMERICAS	30/06/2012	90,599	2012	February	Q1	Allied Biscuit
16	LONG ISLANDS INC	BOTTLES	Michael Jackson	AMERICAS	23/12/2012	17,030	2012	March	Q1	Ankh-Sto Associates
17	LONG ISLANDS INC	BOTTLES	Michael Jackson	AMERICAS	08/12/2012	65,026	2012	April	Q2	Extensive Enterprise
18	LONG ISLANDS INC	BOTTLES	Michael Jackson	AMERICAS	28/10/2012	57,579	2012	May	Q2	Galaxy Corp
19	LONG ISLANDS INC	BOTTLES	Michael Jackson	AMERICAS	28/10/2012	34,338	2012	June	Q2	Globo-Chem
20	LONG ISLANDS INC	BOTTLES	Michael Jackson	AMERICAS	15/09/2012	90,387	2012	July	Q3	Mr. Sparkle
21	LONG ISLANDS INC	BOTTLES	Michael Jackson	AMERICAS	28/10/2012	62,324	2012	August	Q3	Globex Corporation
22	LONG ISLANDS INC	BOTTLES	Michael Jackson	AMERICAS	31/10/2012	28,871	2012	September	Q3	LexCorp

STEP 1: Go to *Developer > Code > Visual Basic*

STEP 2: Paste in your code and **Select Save**. Close the window afterwards.

```vba
Sub PrintWithNarrowMargin()

'Set the Margins to be narrow and print it out
With ActiveSheet.PageSetup
.HeaderMargin = Application.InchesToPoints(0.3)
.FooterMargin = Application.InchesToPoints(0.3)
.LeftMargin = Application.InchesToPoints(0.25)
.RightMargin = Application.InchesToPoints(0.25)
.TopMargin = Application.InchesToPoints(0.75)
.BottomMargin = Application.InchesToPoints(0.75)
End With

Application.Dialogs(xlDialogPrint).Show

End Sub
```

STEP 3: Let us test it out!

Open the sheet containing the data. Go to *Developer > Code > Macros*

Make sure your Macro is selected. Click **Run**.

The Print Dialog is shown. **Click OK** once settings are good.

With just one click, **you have now printed out with narrow margins**!

CUSTOMER	PRODUCTS	SALES PERSON	SALES REGION	ORDER DATE	SALES
LONG ISLANDS INC	SOFT DRINKS	Michael Jackson	AMERICAS	13/04/2012	24,640
LONG ISLANDS INC	SOFT DRINKS	Michael Jackson	AMERICAS	21/12/2012	24,640
LONG ISLANDS INC	SOFT DRINKS	Michael Jackson	AMERICAS	24/12/2012	29,923
LONG ISLANDS INC	SOFT DRINKS	Michael Jackson	AMERICAS	24/12/2012	66,901
LONG ISLANDS INC	SOFT DRINKS	Michael Jackson	AMERICAS	29/12/2012	63,116
LONG ISLANDS INC	SOFT DRINKS	Michael Jackson	AMERICAS	28/06/2012	38,281
LONG ISLANDS INC	SOFT DRINKS	Michael Jackson	AMERICAS	28/06/2012	57,650
LONG ISLANDS INC	SOFT DRINKS	Michael Jackson	AMERICAS	29/06/2012	90,967
LONG ISLANDS INC	SOFT DRINKS	Michael Jackson	AMERICAS	29/06/2012	11,910
LONG ISLANDS INC	SOFT DRINKS	Michael Jackson	AMERICAS	06/07/2012	59,531
LONG ISLANDS INC	SOFT DRINKS	Michael Jackson	AMERICAS	06/07/2012	88,297
LONG ISLANDS INC	SOFT DRINKS	Michael Jackson	AMERICAS	08/09/2012	87,868
LONG ISLANDS INC	BOTTLES	Michael Jackson	AMERICAS	08/09/2012	95,527
LONG ISLANDS INC	BOTTLES	Michael Jackson	AMERICAS	30/06/2012	90,599
LONG ISLANDS INC	BOTTLES	Michael Jackson	AMERICAS	23/12/2012	17,030
LONG ISLANDS INC	BOTTLES	Michael Jackson	AMERICAS	08/12/2012	65,026
LONG ISLANDS INC	BOTTLES	Michael Jackson	AMERICAS	28/10/2012	57,579
LONG ISLANDS INC	BOTTLES	Michael Jackson	AMERICAS	28/10/2012	34,338
LONG ISLANDS INC	BOTTLES	Michael Jackson	AMERICAS	15/09/2012	90,387
LONG ISLANDS INC	BOTTLES	Michael Jackson	AMERICAS	28/10/2012	62,324
LONG ISLANDS INC	BOTTLES	Michael Jackson	AMERICAS	31/10/2012	28,871
LONG ISLANDS INC	BOTTLES	Michael Jackson	AMERICAS	29/12/2012	34,714

WORKBOOK MACROS

Attach Current Workbook into an Email Message

What does it do?

Attach your current workbook into an Outlook email message

Copy Source Code:

```
Sub AttachWorkbookIntoEmailMessage()

Dim OutlookApp As Object
Dim OutlookMail As Object
Set OutlookApp = CreateObject("Outlook.Application")
Set OutlookMail = OutlookApp.CreateItem(0)

'Let us create the email message and display it
'Make sure to change the parameters below
With OutlookMail
.To = "support@myexcelonline.com"
.Subject = "Have a look at this workbook"
.Body = "Hey John, Could you help out on this?"
.Attachments.Add ActiveWorkbook.FullName
.Display
End With

Set OutlookMail = Nothing
Set OutlookApp = Nothing

End Sub
```

Final Result:

Want to quickly **attach your Excel workbook into an email message** with a single click? You can do this with Excel Macros!

STEP 1: Go to *Developer > Code > Visual Basic*

STEP 2: Paste in your code and **Select Save.**

You can change the following fields - **To, Subject and Body** depending on your preferences. These are marked in yellow.

Close the window afterwards.

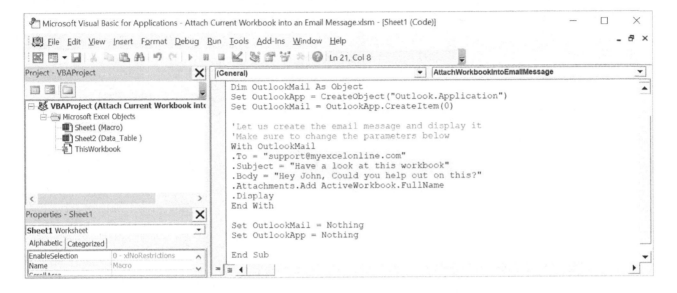

STEP 3: Let us test it out!

Go to ***Developer > Code > Macros***

Make sure your Macro is selected. Click **Run.**

With just one click, **your Excel Workbook is now attached to the email message!**

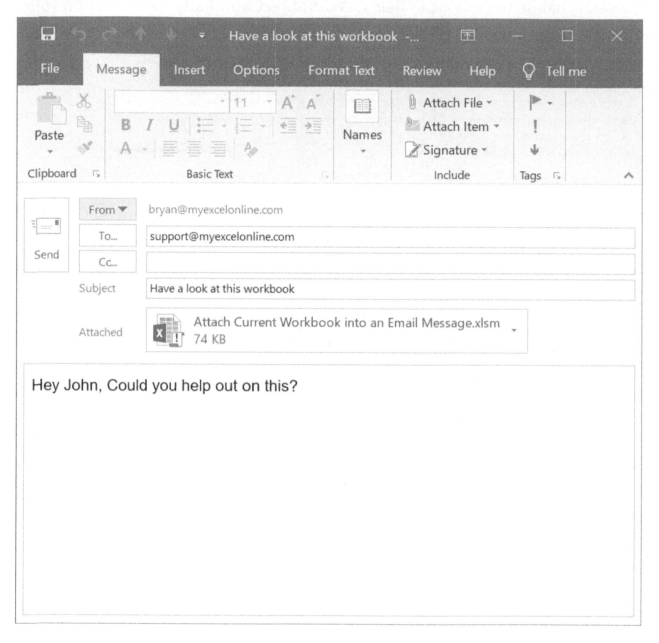

Close All Workbooks and Save Changes

What does it do?

Close all workbooks and save changes for all of them

Copy Source Code:

```
Sub CloseAllWorkbooksAndSaveChanges()
Dim workbook As Workbook
'Loop through all workbooks and close them
For Each workbook In Workbooks
workbook.Close SaveChanges:=True
Next workbook
End Sub
```

Final Result:

Is it a regular occurrence for you to have many Excel workbooks at the same time due to multitasking? We can **close all workbooks and save changes** for all of them using Excel Macros!

To demonstrate this, we have two workbooks currently open:

STEP 1: Go to *Developer > Code > Visual Basic*

STEP 2: Make sure to select **ThisWorkbook**.

Paste in your code and **Select Save**. Close the window afterwards.

STEP 3: Let us test it out!

Go to *Developer > Code > Macros*

Make sure your Macro is selected. Click **Run**.

With just one click, **all of your workbooks are now saved and closed**!

Copy Current Worksheet into a New Workbook

What does it do?

Copies your active worksheet into an entirely new workbook

Copy Source Code:

```
Sub CopyCurrentWorksheetToNewWorkbook()
'Copy the Current Worksheet
ThisWorkbook.ActiveSheet.Copy
Before:=Workbooks.Add.Worksheets(1)
End Sub
```

Final Result:

Have a worksheet that you want to copy into a new worksheet? You can accomplish that with a single line of Excel Macro code! It will **copy the current worksheet into a new workbook**.

STEP 1: Go to *Developer > Code > Visual Basic*

STEP 2: Paste in your code and **Select Save**. Close the window afterwards.

```vba
Sub CopyCurrentWorksheetToNewWorkbook()

'Copy the Current Worksheet
ThisWorkbook.ActiveSheet.Copy Before:=Workbooks.Add.Worksheets(1)

End Sub
```

STEP 3: Let us test it out!

Open the sheet containing the data, this is the one we want to copy to a new worksheet.

	A	B	C	D	E	F	G	H	I	J
1	CUSTOMER	PRODUCTS	SALES PERSON	SALES REGION	ORDER DATE	SALES	FINANCIAL YEAR	SALES MONTH	SALES QTR	CHANNEL PARTNERS
2	LONG ISLANDS INC	SOFT DRINKS	Michael Jackson	AMERICAS	13/04/2012	24,640	2012	January	Q1	Acme, inc.
3	LONG ISLANDS INC	SOFT DRINKS	Michael Jackson	AMERICAS	21/12/2012	24,640	2012	February	Q1	Widget Corp
4	LONG ISLANDS INC	SOFT DRINKS	Michael Jackson	AMERICAS	24/12/2012	29,923	2012	March	Q1	123 Warehousing
5	LONG ISLANDS INC	SOFT DRINKS	Michael Jackson	AMERICAS	24/12/2012	66,901	2012	April	Q2	Demo Company
6	LONG ISLANDS INC	SOFT DRINKS	Michael Jackson	AMERICAS	29/12/2012	63,116	2012	May	Q2	Smith and Co.
7	LONG ISLANDS INC	SOFT DRINKS	Michael Jackson	AMERICAS	28/06/2012	38,281	2012	June	Q2	Foo Bars
8	LONG ISLANDS INC	SOFT DRINKS	Michael Jackson	AMERICAS	28/06/2012	57,650	2012	July	Q3	ABC Telecom
9	LONG ISLANDS INC	SOFT DRINKS	Michael Jackson	AMERICAS	29/06/2012	90,967	2012	August	Q3	Fake Brothers
10	LONG ISLANDS INC	SOFT DRINKS	Michael Jackson	AMERICAS	29/06/2012	11,910	2012	September	Q3	QWERTY Logistics
11	LONG ISLANDS INC	SOFT DRINKS	Michael Jackson	AMERICAS	06/07/2012	59,531	2012	October	Q4	Demo, inc.
12	LONG ISLANDS INC	SOFT DRINKS	Michael Jackson	AMERICAS	06/07/2012	88,297	2012	November	Q4	Sample Company
13	LONG ISLANDS INC	SOFT DRINKS	Michael Jackson	AMERICAS	08/09/2012	87,868	2012	December	Q4	Sample, inc
14	LONG ISLANDS INC	BOTTLES	Michael Jackson	AMERICAS	08/09/2012	95,527	2012	January	Q1	Acme Corp
15	LONG ISLANDS INC	BOTTLES	Michael Jackson	AMERICAS	30/06/2012	90,599	2012	February	Q1	Allied Biscuit
16	LONG ISLANDS INC	BOTTLES	Michael Jackson	AMERICAS	23/12/2012	17,030	2012	March	Q1	Ankh-Sto Associates
17	LONG ISLANDS INC	BOTTLES	Michael Jackson	AMERICAS	08/12/2012	65,026	2012	April	Q2	Extensive Enterprise
18	LONG ISLANDS INC	BOTTLES	Michael Jackson	AMERICAS	28/10/2012	57,579	2012	May	Q2	Galaxy Corp
19	LONG ISLANDS INC	BOTTLES	Michael Jackson	AMERICAS	28/10/2012	34,338	2012	June	Q2	Globo-Chem
20	LONG ISLANDS INC	BOTTLES	Michael Jackson	AMERICAS	15/09/2012	90,387	2012	July	Q3	Mr. Sparkle
21	LONG ISLANDS INC	BOTTLES	Michael Jackson	AMERICAS	28/10/2012	62,324	2012	August	Q3	Globex Corporation
22	LONG ISLANDS INC	BOTTLES	Michael Jackson	AMERICAS	31/10/2012	28,871	2012	September	Q3	LexCorp

Go to *Developer* > *Code* > *Macros*

Make sure your Macro is selected. Click **Run**.

With just one click, **your active worksheet was copied to a new workbook**!

Create a Backup

What does it do?

Creates a backup copy of the spreadsheet in the specified folder

Copy Source Code:

```
Sub CreateBackup()

'Create a backup copy on the specified folder with the date
today included
'Remember to change the folder directory as well
ThisWorkbook.SaveCopyAs Filename:="C:\ChangeMe\" & Format(Date,
"mmddyyyy") & "-" & ThisWorkbook.name

End Sub
```

Final Result:

Have an important spreadsheet that requires frequent backups and snapshots? You can **create a backup** using Excel Macros with a single click!

STEP 1: Go to *Developer > Code > Visual Basic*

STEP 2: Paste in your code and **Select Save**.

Make sure to **change the directory** into a folder that exists for you:

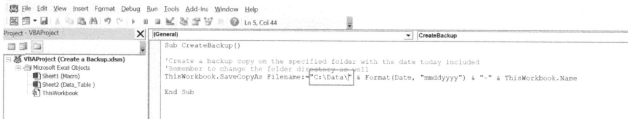

You can see we have changed this to **C:\Data**

Close the window afterwards.

STEP 3: Let us test it out! You can see that we have no files yet in the directory:

Go to *Developer > Code > Macros*

Make sure your Macro is selected. Click **Run**.

With just one click, **you have generated a backup of your current workbook**!

Get the Count of Unsaved Workbooks

What does it do?

Gets the count of unsaved workbooks

Copy Source Code:

```vba
Sub GetCountOfUnsavedWorkbooks()

Dim workbook As Workbook
Dim counter As Integer

For Each workbook In Workbooks
'Count the unsaved workbooks
If workbook.Saved = False Then
counter = counter + 1
End If
Next workbook

MsgBox "You have " & counter & " unsaved workbook(s)"

End Sub
```

Final Result:

Have many workbooks open and need a quick survey of unsaved files? Excel Macros will get the **count of unsaved workbooks** for you!

We have 2 workbooks open that have unsaved changes:

STEP 1: In any one of the workbooks, go to *Developer > Code > Visual Basic*

STEP 2: Paste in your code and **Select Save**. Close the window afterwards.

```
Sub GetCountOfUnsavedWorkbooks()

Dim workbook As workbook
Dim counter As Integer

For Each workbook In Workbooks
'Count the unsaved workbooks
If workbook.Saved = False Then
counter = counter + 1
End If
Next workbook

MsgBox "You have " & counter & " unsaved workbook(s)"

End Sub
```

STEP 3: Let us test it out!

Go to *Developer > Code > Macros*

Make sure your Macro is selected. Click **Run**.

With just one click, **you now have the number of unsaved workbooks**!

Set the Active Worksheet

What does it do?

Activates the worksheet designated in your Excel Macro when you open the Excel file.

Copy Source Code:

```
'Ensure this is saved inside the Workbook
Sub Workbook_Open()
'This activates when you open the workbook.
'Change the sheet name to your desired sheet.
Sheets("Europe").Activate
End Sub
```

Final Result:

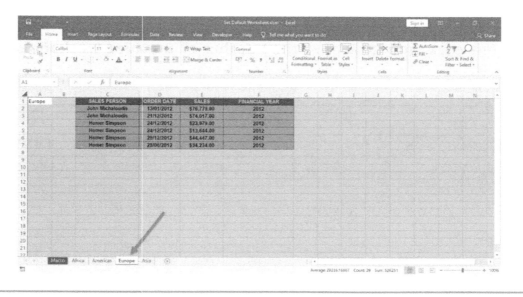

Want to try something cool when your users open your workbook? **Set a default worksheet** to open using Excel Macros!

This is our list of worksheets, we want it to default to **Europe** when we open the workbook.

STEP 1: Go to *Developer > Code > Visual Basic*

STEP 2: Paste in your code and **Select Save**. Make sure it is saved in **ThisWorkbook**.

You can change the Sheet Name in the code (e.g. "Europe") if you want a different default worksheet.

Close the window afterwards.

```vba
'Ensure this is saved inside the Workbook
Sub Workbook_Open()

'This activates when you open the workbook
Sheets("Europe").Activate

End Sub
```

STEP 3: Let us test it out! Close your workbook. Then open it up.

Your Macro will execute once you open the workbook. Now you can see your **new default worksheet**!

Show a Closing Message

What does it do?

Shows a closing message once the Excel Workbook is closed

Copy Source Code:

```
'Ensure this is saved inside the Workbook
Sub Workbook_BeforeClose(Cancel As Boolean)

MsgBox "Thanks for downloading this and view more tutorials at
MyExcelOnline.com"

End Sub
```

Final Result:

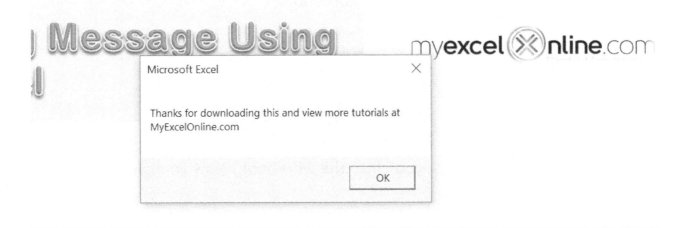

We have a cool trick to try out using Excel Macros, we can **show a closing message** to thank your user once they close the spreadsheet.

STEP 1: Go to *Developer > Code > Visual Basic*

STEP 2: Paste in your code and **Select Save**. Make sure it is saved in **ThisWorkbook**.

You can change the text to show in the closing message as well.

Close the window afterwards.

STEP 3: Let us test it out! Close your workbook.

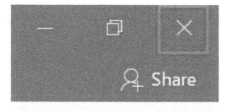

Your Macro will execute once you close the workbook. Now you can see your **closing message**!

Show a Welcome Message

What does it do?

Shows a welcome message whenever you open the workbook

Copy Source Code:

```
'Ensure this is saved inside the Workbook
Sub Workbook_Open()

MsgBox "Thanks for downloading this and view more tutorials at
MyExcelOnline.com"

End Sub
```

Final Result:

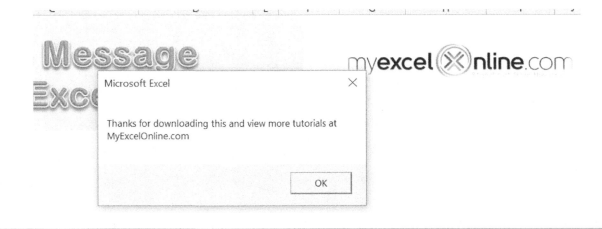

Want to try something cool when your users open your workbook? **Show a welcome message** using Excel Macros!

STEP 1: Go to *Developer > Code > Visual Basic*

STEP 2: Paste in your code and **Select Save**. Make sure it is saved in **ThisWorkbook**.

You can change the text to show in the welcome message as well.

Close the window afterwards.

STEP 3: Let us test it out! Close your workbook. Then open it up:

Your Macro will execute once you open the workbook. Now you can see your **welcome message**!

WORKSHEET MACROS

Delete All Other Worksheets

What does it do?

Deletes all other worksheets except the active worksheet

Copy Source Code:

```
Sub DeleteAllOtherWorksheets()

Dim worksheet As Worksheet
'Loop through the worksheets
For Each worksheet In ThisWorkbook.Worksheets
'Delete the sheet if it's not the active sheet
If worksheet.name <> ThisWorkbook.ActiveSheet.name Then
Application.DisplayAlerts = False
worksheet.Delete
Application.DisplayAlerts = True
End If

Next worksheet
End Sub
```

Final Result:

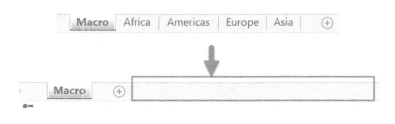

Wanted to **delete all other worksheets** in a single click? You can do that using Macros in Excel!

These are the worksheets in the file:

STEP 1: Go to *Developer > Code > Visual Basic*

STEP 2: Paste in your code and **Select Save**. Close the window afterwards.

```vba
Sub DeleteAllOtherWorksheets()

Dim worksheet As worksheet

'Loop through the worksheets
For Each worksheet In ThisWorkbook.Worksheets

'Delete the sheet if it's not the active sheet
If worksheet.Name <> ThisWorkbook.ActiveSheet.Name Then
Application.DisplayAlerts = False
worksheet.Delete
Application.DisplayAlerts = True
End If

Next worksheet

End Sub
```

STEP 3: Let us test it out!

Select the worksheet that you do not want to be deleted. Go to *Developer > Code > Macros*

Make sure your Macro is selected. Click **Run**.

With just one click, **all of the other worksheets are now deleted**!

Delete Blank Worksheets

What does it do?

Deletes all worksheets that are blank

Copy Source Code:

```vba
Sub DeleteBlankWorksheets()
Dim wsheet As Worksheet
On Error Resume Next
Application.DisplayAlerts = False
Application.ScreenUpdating = False
'Loop through all worksheets and delete the blank ones
For Each wsheet In Application.Worksheets
If Application.WorksheetFunction.CountA(wsheet.UsedRange) = 0
Then
wsheet.Delete
End If
Next
Application.DisplayAlerts = True
Application.ScreenUpdating = True
End Sub
```

Final Result:

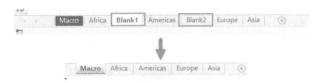

Want to do some cleanup and delete the empty worksheets in your workbook? Excel Macros will make this happen in a click and **delete blank worksheets**!

These are our worksheets, the ones enclosed in red are blank worksheets:

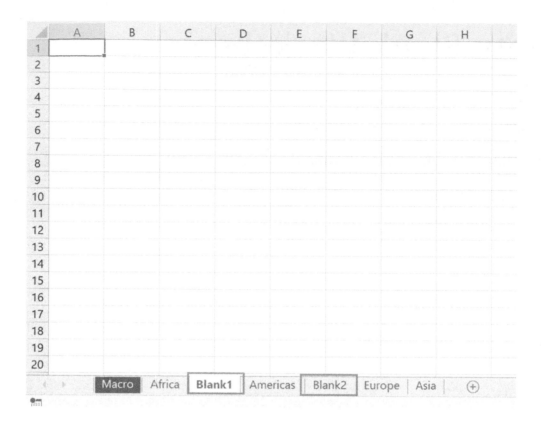

STEP 1: Go to *Developer > Code > Visual Basic*

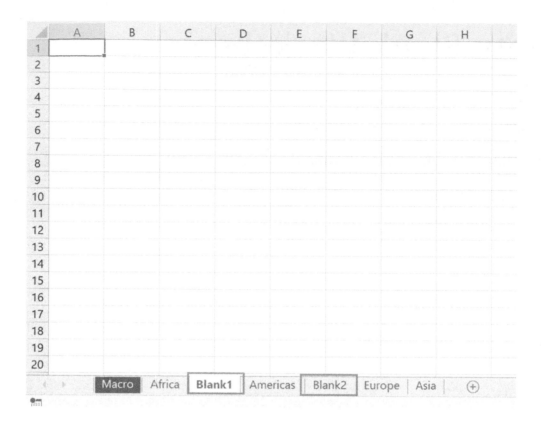

STEP 2: Paste in your code and **Select Save**. Close the window afterwards.

```vba
Sub DeleteBlankWorksheets()

Dim worksheet As worksheet

On Error Resume Next
Application.DisplayAlerts = False
Application.ScreenUpdating = False

'Loop through all worksheets and delete the blank ones
For Each worksheet In Application.Worksheets
If Application.WorksheetFunction.CountA(worksheet.UsedRange) = 0 Then
worksheet.Delete
End If
Next

Application.DisplayAlerts = True
Application.ScreenUpdating = True

End Sub
```

Delete Blank Worksheets

WORKSHEET MACROS

STEP 3: Let us test it out!

Go to **Developer > Code > Macros**

Make sure your Macro is selected. Click **Run.**

With just one click, **all of the blank worksheets are now deleted**!

Hide All Other Worksheets

What does it do?

Hide all other worksheets except the active worksheet

Copy Source Code:

```
Sub HideAllOtherWorksheets()

Dim worksheet As Worksheet

'Loop through the worksheets
For Each worksheet In ThisWorkbook.Worksheets
'Hide the sheet if it's not the active sheet
If worksheet.Name <> ThisWorkbook.ActiveSheet.Name Then
worksheet.Visible = xlSheetHidden
End If
Next worksheet

End Sub
```

Final Result:

Want to hide all worksheets except your active one? You can **hide all other worksheets using Macros in Excel**!

STEP 1: Go to *Developer > Code > Visual Basic*

STEP 2: Paste in your code and **Select Save**. Close the window afterwards.

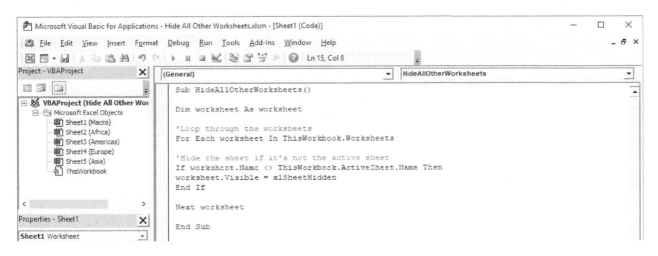

STEP 3: Let us test it out! These are all of our worksheets that we want to hide.

	A	B	C	D	E	F	G
1	Africa		SALES PERSON	ORDER DATE	SALES	FINANCIAL YEAR	
2			Michael Jackson	10/31/2013	$16,853.00	2013	
3			John Michaloudis	10/28/2013	$35,796.00	2013	
4			John Michaloudis	10/31/2013	$64,825.00	2013	
5			John Michaloudis	11/3/2013	$17,929.00	2013	
6			Homer Simpson	12/1/2013	$50,134.00	2013	
7			Homer Simpson	10/31/2013	$95,705.00	2013	
8							
9							
10							
11							
12							
13							
14							
15							
16							
17							
18							
19							
20							
21							
22							
23							

Macro | **Africa** | Americas | Europe | Asia | ⊕

Open the sheet containing the data. Go to *Developer > Code > Macros*

Make sure your Macro is selected. Click **Run**.

With just one click, **all of the other worksheets are all hidden**!

Insert Multiple Worksheets

What does it do?

Insert multiple worksheets based on the user input of the number of sheets

Copy Source Code:

```
Sub InsertMultipleWorksheets()

Dim numOfSheets As Integer

'Get the number of sheets from the user
numOfSheets = InputBox("Enter number of sheets to insert",
"Enter number of sheets")
'Add the additional sheets after the current active sheet
Sheets.Add After:=ActiveSheet, Count:=numOfSheets

End Sub
```

Final Result:

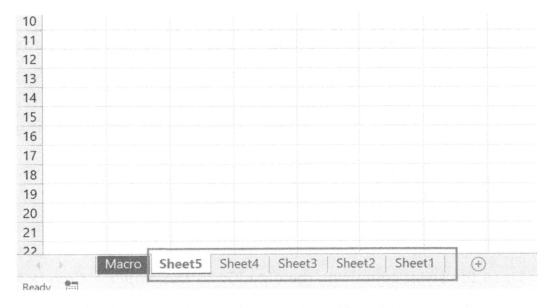

Have multiple blank worksheets to insert? You can **insert multiple worksheets using Excel Macros!**

We only have one worksheet so far, let us work out our magic!

STEP 1: Go to *Developer > Code > Visual Basic*

STEP 2: Paste in your code and **Select Save**. Close the window afterwards.

```vba
Sub InsertMultipleWorksheets()

Dim numOfSheets As Integer

'Get the number of sheets from the user
numOfSheets = InputBox("Enter number of sheets to insert", "Enter number of sheets")
'Add the additional sheets after the current active sheet
Sheets.Add After:=ActiveSheet, Count:=numOfSheets

End Sub
```

STEP 3: Open the sheet containing the data. Go to *Developer > Code > Macros*

Make sure your Macro is selected. Click **Run**.

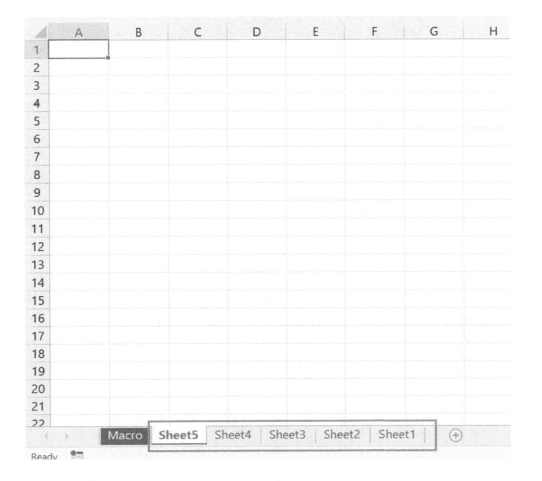

Let us try out adding 5 worksheets. **Click OK.**

With just one click, **you have inserted multiple worksheets**!

Protect Active Worksheet

What does it do?

Protects the active worksheet with the password specified by the user

Copy Source Code:

```
Sub ProtectActiveWorksheet()
Dim pword As String
'Get the password from the user
pword = InputBox("Enter a Password to Protect the Worksheet")
'Protect the Active Worksheet
ActiveSheet.Protect pword, True, True
End Sub
```

Final Result:

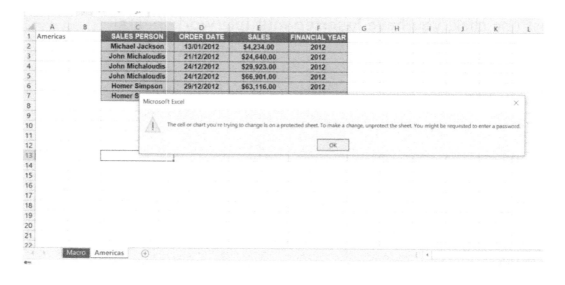

Wanted to protect your active worksheet programmatically? We will show you how to **protect the active worksheet** using Macros in Excel!

Here are our worksheets:

STEP 1: Go to *Developer > Code > Visual Basic*

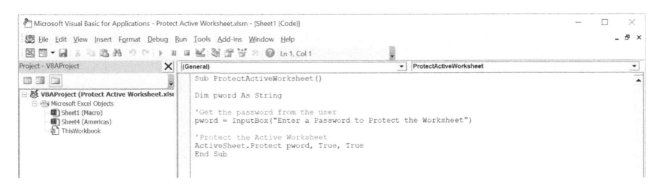

STEP 2: Paste in your code and **Select Save**. Close the window afterwards.

```
Sub ProtectActiveWorksheet()

Dim pword As String

'Get the password from the user
pword = InputBox("Enter a Password to Protect the Worksheet")

'Protect the Active Worksheet
ActiveSheet.Protect pword, True, True
End Sub
```

STEP 3: Let us test it out!

Select your sheet to protect. For our example let us select the **Americas** worksheet.

Go to *Developer > Code > Macros*

Make sure your Macro is selected. Click **Run**.

Type in the password to protect the worksheet. **Click OK.**

Try editing your worksheet. You can verify that **the worksheet is now protected**!

Unprotect Active Worksheet

What does it do?

Unprotect the active worksheet

Copy Source Code:

```
Sub UnprotectActiveWorksheet()

Dim pword As String

'Get the password from the user
pword = InputBox("Enter a Password to Unprotect the Worksheet")

'Unprotect the Active Worksheet
ActiveSheet.Unprotect pword
End Sub
```

Final Result:

	A	B	C	D	
1	CUSTOMER	PRODUCTS	SALES PERSON	SALES REGION	
2	LONG ISLANDS INC	CHANGED IT	Michael Jackson	AMERICAS	
3	LONG ISLANDS INC	SOFT DRINKS	Michael Jackson	AMERICAS	
4	LONG ISLANDS INC	SOFT DRINKS	Michael Jackson	AMERICAS	
5	LONG ISLANDS INC	SOFT DRINKS	Michael Jackson	AMERICAS	
6	LONG ISLANDS INC	SOFT DRINKS	Michael Jackson	AMERICAS	
7	LONG ISLANDS INC	SOFT DRINKS	Michael Jackson	AMERICAS	
8	LONG ISLANDS INC	SOFT DRINKS	Michael Jackson	AMERICAS	

Ever wondered how to unprotect the active worksheet using code? Let us show you how to **unprotect the active worksheet** with Excel Macros!

This is our worksheet, same as from the previous example worksheet of the **Protect Active Worksheet** tutorial.

It is locked at the moment, with the same password: MyExcelOnline.

12	LONG ISLANDS INC	SOFT DRINKS	Michael Jackson	AMERICAS	06/07/2012	88,297	2012	November	Q4
13	LONG ISLANDS INC	SOFT DRINKS	Michael Jackson	AMERICAS	08/09/2012	87,868	2012	December	Q4
14	LONG								Q1
15	LONG								Q1
16	LONG								Q1
17	LONG								Q2
18	LONG								Q2
19	LONG								Q2
20	LONG ISLANDS INC	BOTTLES	Michael Jackson	AMERICAS	15/09/2012	90,387	2012	July	Q3
21	LONG ISLANDS INC	BOTTLES	Michael Jackson	AMERICAS	28/10/2012	62,324	2012	August	Q3
22	LONG ISLANDS INC	BOTTLES	Michael Jackson	AMERICAS	31/10/2012	28,871	2012	September	Q3

Microsoft Excel

The cell or chart you're trying to change is on a protected sheet. To make a change, unprotect the sheet. You might be requested to enter a password.

OK

Macro   Data_Table

STEP 1: Go to *Developer > Code > Visual Basic*

File   Home   Insert   Page Layout   Formulas   Data   Review   View   Developer   Help   Tell me what you want to

Visual Basic   Macros   Use Relative References   Macro Security   — Code
Add-ins   Excel Add-ins   COM Add-ins   — Add-ins
Insert   Design Mode   Properties   View Code   Run Dialog   — Controls
Source   Map Properties   Expansion Packs   Refresh Data   Import   Export   — XML

STEP 2: Paste in your code and **Select Save**. Close the window afterwards.

Microsoft Visual Basic for Applications - Unprotect Active Worksheet.xlsm - [Sheet1 (Code)]

File   Edit   View   Insert   Format   Debug   Run   Tools   Add-Ins   Window   Help

Ln 10, Col 8

Project - VBAProject

VBAProject (Unprotect Active Worksheet.)
  Microsoft Excel Objects
    Sheet1 (Macro)
    Sheet2 (Data_Table)
    ThisWorkbook

(General)   UnprotectActiveWorksheet

```vba
Sub UnprotectActiveWorksheet()

Dim pword As String

'Get the password from the user
pword = InputBox("Enter a Password to Unprotect the Worksheet")

'Unprotect the Active Worksheet
ActiveSheet.Unprotect pword
End Sub
```

STEP 3: Let us test it out!

Open the protected sheet. Go to *Developer > Code > Macros*

Make sure your Macro is selected. Click **Run**.

Type in the password to unlock the sheet. **Click OK.**

Microsoft Excel ✕

Enter a Password to Unprotect the Worksheet

OK

Cancel

MyExcelOnline|

Now your sheet **is now unprotected**! We can now try editing the sheet.

	A	B	C	D	
1	**CUSTOMER**	**PRODUCTS**	**SALES PERSON**	**SALES REGION**	**ORDE**
2	LONG ISLANDS INC	CHANGED IT	Michael Jackson	AMERICAS	13/0
3	LONG ISLANDS INC	SOFT DRINKS	Michael Jackson	AMERICAS	21/1
4	LONG ISLANDS INC	SOFT DRINKS	Michael Jackson	AMERICAS	24/1
5	LONG ISLANDS INC	SOFT DRINKS	Michael Jackson	AMERICAS	24/1
6	LONG ISLANDS INC	SOFT DRINKS	Michael Jackson	AMERICAS	29/1
7	LONG ISLANDS INC	SOFT DRINKS	Michael Jackson	AMERICAS	28/0
8	LONG ISLANDS INC	SOFT DRINKS	Michael Jackson	AMERICAS	28/0
9	LONG ISLANDS INC	SOFT DRINKS	Michael Jackson	AMERICAS	29/0
10	LONG ISLANDS INC	SOFT DRINKS	Michael Jackson	AMERICAS	29/0
11	LONG ISLANDS INC	SOFT DRINKS	Michael Jackson	AMERICAS	06/0
12	LONG ISLANDS INC	SOFT DRINKS	Michael Jackson	AMERICAS	06/0
13	LONG ISLANDS INC	SOFT DRINKS	Michael Jackson	AMERICAS	08/0
14	LONG ISLANDS INC	BOTTLES	Michael Jackson	AMERICAS	08/0
15	LONG ISLANDS INC	BOTTLES	Michael Jackson	AMERICAS	30/0
16	LONG ISLANDS INC	BOTTLES	Michael Jackson	AMERICAS	23/1
17	LONG ISLANDS INC	BOTTLES	Michael Jackson	AMERICAS	08/1
18	LONG ISLANDS INC	BOTTLES	Michael Jackson	AMERICAS	28/1
19	LONG ISLANDS INC	BOTTLES	Michael Jackson	AMERICAS	28/1
20	LONG ISLANDS INC	BOTTLES	Michael Jackson	AMERICAS	15/0
21	LONG ISLANDS INC	BOTTLES	Michael Jackson	AMERICAS	28/1
22	LONG ISLANDS INC	BOTTLES	Michael Jackson	AMERICAS	31/1

Macro Data_Table ⊕

Protect All Cells With Formulas

What does it do?

Locks all of the cells with formulas

Copy Source Code:

```
Sub ProtectAllCellsWithFormulas()
'Lock all of the cells with formulas in one go
With ActiveSheet
.Unprotect
.Cells.Locked = False
.Cells.SpecialCells(xlCellTypeFormulas).Locked = True
.Protect AllowDeletingRows:=True
End With
End Sub
```

Final Result:

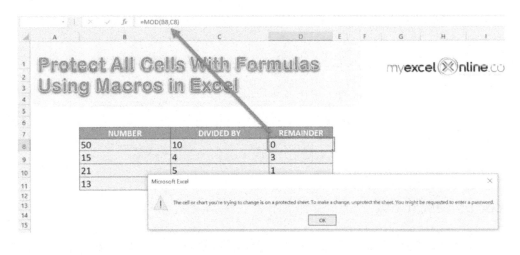

We usually have a lot of cells with formulas in our worksheets. Wanted to protect these separately? You can **protect all cells with formulas** using Excel Macros!

These are our cells with formulas:

NUMBER	DIVIDED BY	REMAINDER
50	10	0
15	4	3
21	5	1
13	5	3

STEP 1: Go to **_Developer > Code > Visual Basic_**

STEP 2: Paste in your code and **Select Save**. Close the window afterwards.

```vba
Sub ProtectAllCellsWithFormulas()

'Lock all of the cells with formulas in one go
With ActiveSheet
.Unprotect
.Cells.Locked = False
.Cells.SpecialCells(xlCellTypeFormulas).Locked = True
.Protect AllowDeletingRows:=True
End With

End Sub
```

STEP 3: Let us test it out!

Open the sheet containing the data. Go to **_Developer > Code > Macros_**

Make sure your Macro is selected. Click **Run**.

With just one click, **all of the cells with formulas are now protected**!

Protect All Worksheets

What does it do?

Protects all worksheets with the user-given password

Copy Source Code:

```
Sub ProtectAllWorksheets()

Dim worksheet As Worksheet
Dim pword As String

'Get the password from the user
pword = InputBox("Enter a Password to Protect All Worksheets",
"Password")

'Loop through the worksheets and protect all of them
For Each worksheet In ActiveWorkbook.Worksheets
worksheet.Protect Password:=pword
Next worksheet

End Sub
```

Final Result:

You can **protect all worksheets** using Macros in Excel! You will ask the user for the password then use it to protect all of the worksheets in the file.

This is our list of worksheets:

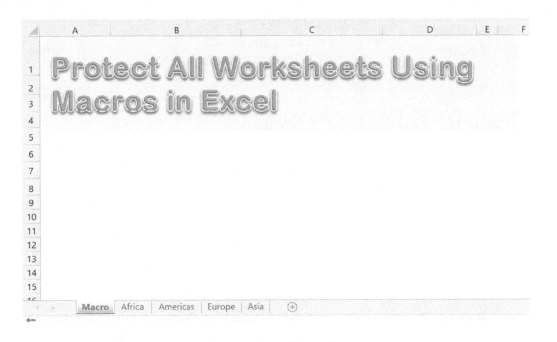

STEP 1: Go to **Developer > Code > Visual Basic**

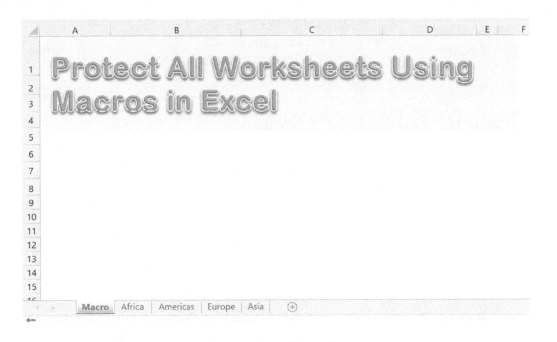

STEP 2: Paste in your code and **Select Save.** Close the window afterwards.

```
Sub ProtectAllWorksheets()

Dim Worksheet As Worksheet
Dim pword As String

'Get the password from the user
pword = InputBox("Enter a Password to Protect All Worksheets", "Password")

'Loop through the worksheets and protect all of them
For Each Worksheet In ActiveWorkbook.Worksheets
Worksheet.Protect Password:=pword
Next Worksheet

End Sub
```

STEP 3: Let us test it out!

Go to **Developer > Code > Macros**

Make sure your Macro is selected. Click **Run**.

Type in a password and **click OK**.

With just one click, **all of your worksheets are now protected**!

	A	B	C	D	E	F	G	H	I	J	K	L
1	Africa		SALES PERSON	ORDER DATE	SALES	FINANCIAL YEAR						
2			Michael Jackson	31/10/2013	$16,853.00	2013						
3			John Michaloudis	28/10/2013	$35,796.00	2013						
4			John Michaloudis	31/10/2013	$64,825.00	2013						
5			John Michaloudis	03/11/2013	$17,929.00	2013						
6			Homer Simpson									
7			Homer Simpson									

Microsoft Excel ×

⚠ The cell or chart you're trying to change is on a protected sheet. To make a change, unprotect the sheet. You might be requested to enter a password.

OK

Macro | Africa | Americas | Europe | Asia | ⊕

Ready

Save Each Worksheet as a PDF File

What does it do?

Save each worksheet as a PDF file

Copy Source Code:

```
Sub SaveEachWorksheetAsPdfFile()

Dim worksheet As Worksheet

'Loop through all of the worksheets
'Remember to change the folder directory as well
For Each worksheet In Worksheets
worksheet.ExportAsFixedFormat xlTypePDF, "C:\ChangeMe\" &
worksheet.Name & ".pdf"
Next worksheet

End Sub
```

Final Result:

Name	Type	Size
Africa	PDF File	33 KB
Americas	PDF File	33 KB
Asia	PDF File	33 KB
Europe	PDF File	33 KB
Macro	PDF File	248 KB

Want to **export and save each worksheet as a PDF file**? You can do that with a single click using Excel Macros!

We want to export these worksheets into pdf files:

STEP 1: Go to *Developer > Code > Visual Basic*

STEP 2: Paste in your code and **Select Save**.

Remember to **change the directory** on where you want to save the pdf files. Close the window afterwards.

STEP 3: Let us test it out!

Open the sheet containing the data. Go to *Developer > Code > Macros*

Make sure your Macro is selected. Click **Run**.

Let us check the folder, and you will see these worksheets:

Name	Type	Size
Africa	PDF File	33 KB
Americas	PDF File	33 KB
Asia	PDF File	33 KB
Europe	PDF File	33 KB
Macro	PDF File	248 KB

Let us open one of the files, and it is exactly the same as the one in the workbook!

SALES PERSON	ORDER DATE	SALES	FINANCIAL YEAR
Michael Jackson	31/10/2013	$16,853.00	2013
John Michaloudis	28/10/2013	$35,796.00	2013
John Michaloudis	31/10/2013	$64,825.00	2013
John Michaloudis	03/11/2013	$17,929.00	2013
Homer Simpson	01/12/2013	$50,134.00	2013
Homer Simpson	31/10/2013	$95,705.00	2013

Sort All Worksheets Alphabetically

What does it do?

Sort all worksheets by name alphabetically

Copy Source Code:

```
Sub SortAllWorksheetsByName()

Dim i As Integer
Dim j As Integer
'We use two loops to sort the sheets in ascending order
For i = 1 To Sheets.Count
For j = 1 To Sheets.Count - 1
If UCase$(Sheets(j).Name) > UCase$(Sheets(j + 1).Name) Then
Sheets(j).Move After:=Sheets(j + 1)
End If
Next j
Next i
End Sub
```

Final Result:

Have a lot of worksheets but the worksheet names are arranged in a random order? It will be a pain moving the sheets one by one to sort them out! You can **sort all worksheets by name using Macros in Excel!**

This is our worksheet ordering:

STEP 1: Go to *Developer > Code > Visual Basic*

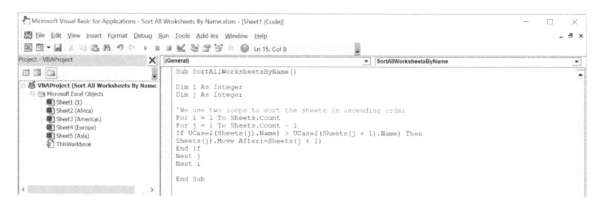

STEP 2: Paste in your code and **Select Save**. Close the window afterwards.

```
Sub SortAllWorksheetsByName()

Dim i As Integer
Dim j As Integer

'We use two loops to sort the sheets in ascending order
For i = 1 To Sheets.Count
For j = 1 To Sheets.Count - 1
If UCase$(Sheets(j).Name) > UCase$(Sheets(j + 1).Name) Then
Sheets(j).Move After:=Sheets(j + 1)
End If
Next j
Next i

End Sub
```

STEP 3: Let us test it out!

Open the sheet containing the data. Go to *Developer > Code > Macros*

Make sure your Macro is selected. Click **Run**.

With just one click, **all of the worksheets are now sorted alphabetically**!

Unhide All Hidden Rows and Columns

What does it do?

Shows all hidden rows and columns

Copy Source Code:

```
Sub UnhideAllHiddenRowsAndColumns()
'Unhide all hidden rows and columns
Columns.EntireColumn.Hidden = False
Rows.EntireRow.Hidden = False
End Sub
```

Final Result:

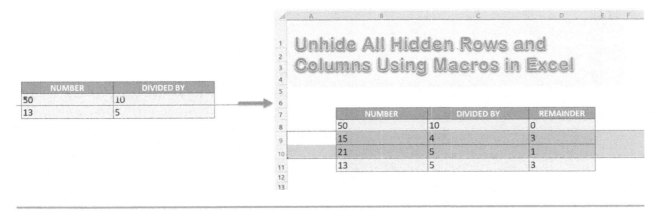

We usually hide either rows or columns if we use them as helper cells to calculate something. If we lose track of which ones we have hidden, we can quickly **unhide all hidden rows and columns** using Excel Macros!

This is our original table:

NUMBER	DIVIDED BY	REMAINDER
50	10	0
15	4	3
21	5	1
13	5	3

Now let us **hide 2 rows and 1 column**:

NUMBER	DIVIDED BY
50	10
13	5

STEP 1: Go to ***Developer > Code > Visual Basic***

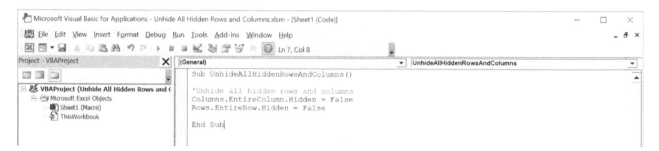

STEP 2: Paste in your code and **Select Save**. Close the window afterwards.

```
Sub UnhideAllHiddenRowsAndColumns()

'Unhide all hidden rows and columns
Columns.EntireColumn.Hidden = False
Rows.EntireRow.Hidden = False

End Sub
```

STEP 3: Let us test it out!

Open the sheet containing the data. Go to ***Developer > Code > Macros***

Make sure your Macro is selected. Click **Run**.

With just one click, **all of the hidden rows and columns are now shown**!

Unhide All Worksheets

What does it do?

Unhide all worksheets

Copy Source Code:

```
Sub UnhideAllWorksheets()
Dim worksheet As Worksheet
'Loop through all worksheets and set them to visible
For Each worksheet In ActiveWorkbook.Worksheets
worksheet.Visible = xlSheetVisible
Next worksheet
End Sub
```

Final Result:

Want to unhide all worksheets with just a single click? You can **unhide all worksheets using Macros in Excel**!

STEP 1: Go to *Developer > Code > Visual Basic*

STEP 2: Paste in your code and **Select Save**. Close the window afterwards.

```
Microsoft Visual Basic for Applications - Unhide All Worksheets.xlsm - [Sheet1 (Code)]

File  Edit  View  Insert  Format  Debug  Run  Tools  Add-Ins  Window  Help
                                                            Ln 10, Col 8

Project - VBAProject                    (General)                    UnhideAllWorksheets

VBAProject (Unhide All Worksh          Sub UnhideAllWorksheets()
  Microsoft Excel Objects
    Sheet1 (Macro)                     Dim worksheet As worksheet
    Sheet2 (Africa)
    Sheet3 (Americas)                  'Loop through all worksheets and set them to visible
    Sheet4 (Europe)                    For Each worksheet In ActiveWorkbook.Worksheets
    Sheet5 (Asia)                      worksheet.Visible = xlSheetVisible
    ThisWorkbook                       Next worksheet

                                       End Sub
```

STEP 3: Let us test it out! This is the only tab we are seeing at the moment.

Open the sheet containing the data. Go to *Developer > Code > Macros*

Make sure your Macro is selected. Click **Run**.

```
Macro                                           ?    ×

Macro name:
Sheet1.UnhideAllWorksheets              ↑       Run

Sheet1.UnhideAllWorksheets                      Step Into

                                                Edit

                                                Create

                                                Delete

                                                Options...

Macros in:  All Open Workbooks
Description

                                                Cancel
```

With just one click, **all of the hidden worksheets are now shown!**

	A	B	C	D	E	F	G
1	Africa		SALES PERSON	ORDER DATE	SALES	FINANCIAL YEAR	
2			Michael Jackson	10/31/2013	$16,853.00	2013	
3			John Michaloudis	10/28/2013	$35,796.00	2013	
4			John Michaloudis	10/31/2013	$64,825.00	2013	
5			John Michaloudis	11/3/2013	$17,929.00	2013	
6			Homer Simpson	12/1/2013	$50,134.00	2013	
7			Homer Simpson	10/31/2013	$95,705.00	2013	
8							
9							
10							
11							
12							
13							
14							
15							
16							
17							
18							
19							
20							
21							
22							
23							

Macro | Africa | Americas | Europe | Asia | ⊕

Ready

ADVANCED MACROS

Convert Selected Range into an Image

What does it do?

Converts your selected range into an image

Copy Source Code:

```vba
'Make sure you have a selected range first
Sub ConvertSelectedRangeIntoAnImage()

Selection.Copy
'Paste the selection as an image
ActiveSheet.Pictures.Paste.Select

End Sub
```

Final Result:

Did you know that even Excel Macros you can create screenshots with it? That's right, let us use Excel Macros to **convert your selected range into an image**!

This is our target, we want to convert this header into an image!

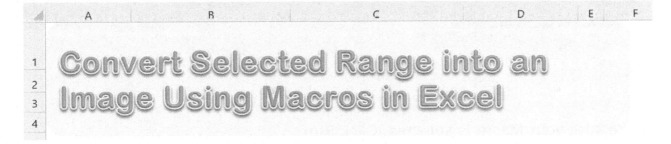

Convert Selected Range into an Image Using Macros in Excel

STEP 1: Go to ***Developer > Code > Visual Basic***

STEP 2: Paste in your code and **Select Save**. Close the window afterwards.

```vba
'Make sure you have a selected range first
Sub ConvertSelectedRangeIntoAnImage()

Selection.Copy
'Paste the selection as an image
ActiveSheet.Pictures.Paste.Select

End Sub
```

STEP 3: Let us test it out!

Open the sheet containing the header. Make sure the header is highlighted. Go to ***Developer > Code > Macros***

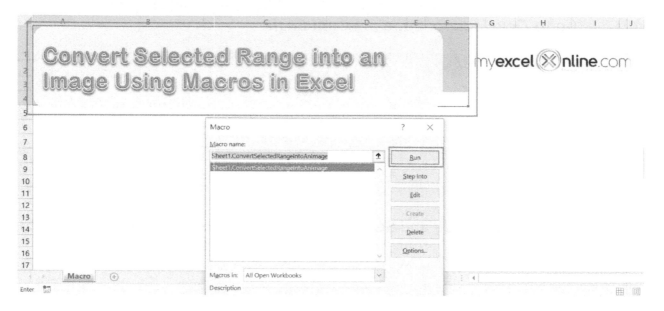

Make sure your Macro is selected. Click **Run**.

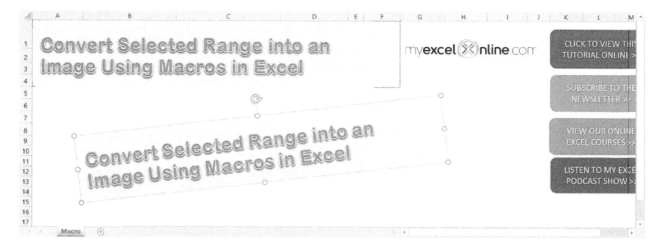

With just one click, **you have now created a screenshot using Macros**! You can even rotate it or resize it now.

Convert Text into Speech

What does it do?

Reads your selection out aloud

Copy Source Code:

```
'Make sure you have a selection of text
Sub ConvertTextIntoSpeech()
'Hear your words spoken out load!
Selection.Speak
End Sub
```

Final Result:

Did you know that Excel can actually talk? That's right, we can use Excel Macros to **convert text into speech.** We can instruct Excel to read text aloud to us!

These are our sentences that we want to hear read aloud:

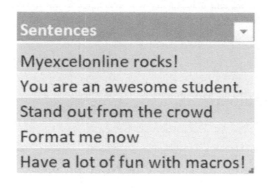

STEP 1: Go to *Developer > Code > Visual Basic*

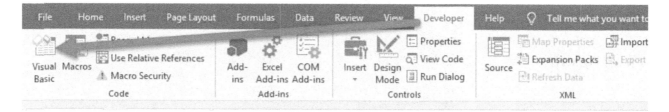

STEP 2: Paste in your code and **Select Save**. Close the window afterwards.

```
'Make sure you have a selection of text
Sub ConvertTextIntoSpeech()

'Hear your words spoken out load!
Selection.Speak

End Sub
```

STEP 3: Let us test it out!

Open the sheet containing the data. Make sure your sentences are highlighted.
Go to *Developer > Code > Macros*

Make sure your Macro is selected. Click **Run**.

With just one click, **you can hear your text being read aloud**! Make sure your sounds are turned on 😊

Create Table of Contents

What does it do?

Creates a table of contents for all of the worksheets

Copy Source Code:

```vba
Sub CreateTableOfContents()

Dim counter As Long

On Error Resume Next
Application.DisplayAlerts = False
'If this worksheet already exists, let us redo this
Worksheets("Table of Contents").Delete
Application.DisplayAlerts = True
On Error GoTo 0

'Let us add a new worksheet as our Table of Contents
ThisWorkbook.Sheets.Add Before:=ThisWorkbook.Worksheets(1)
ActiveSheet.Name = "Table of Contents"

'Let us enumerate all of the worksheets in our ToC
For counter = 1 To Sheets.Count
'This will add one hyperlink for the specific sheet
ActiveSheet.Hyperlinks.Add _
Anchor:=ActiveSheet.Cells(counter, 1), _
Address:="", _
SubAddress:="'" & Sheets(counter).Name & "'!A1", _
ScreenTip:=Sheets(counter).Name, _
TextToDisplay:=Sheets(counter).Name

Next counter

End Sub
```

Final Result:

	A	B	C	D	E	F	G	H	I	J
1	Table of Contents									
2	Macro									
3	Data_Table									
4	Africa									
5	Americas									
6	Europe									
7	Asia									
8										
9										
10										
11										
12										
13										
14										
15										
16										
17										
18										
19										
20										
21										
22										

Table of Contents | Macro | Data_Table | Africa | Americas | Europe | Asia | ⊕

This is one of the most fun and coolest Macros that you can use. If you have a lot of worksheets, it is very annoying to scroll left to right to find out what other worksheets you have. We can use Excel Macros to **create a table of contents** for easy navigation!

This is our list of worksheets:

Macro | Data_Table | Africa | Americas | Europe | Asia | ⊕

STEP 1: Go to *Developer > Code > Visual Basic*

File | Home | Insert | Page Layout | Formulas | Data | Review | View | Developer | Help | ♡ Tell me what you want to

Visual Basic | Macros | Record... | Use Relative References | ⚠ Macro Security | Add-ins | Excel Add-ins | COM Add-ins | Insert | Design Mode | ▦ Properties | ▤ View Code | ▤ Run Dialog | Source | ▤ Map Properties | ▤ Expansion Packs | ▤ Refresh Data | ▤ Import | ▤ Export

Code | Add-ins | Controls | XML

STEP 2: Paste in your code and **Select Save**. Close the window afterwards.

```vba
Sub CreateTableOfContents()

Dim counter As Long

On Error Resume Next
Application.DisplayAlerts = False
'If this worksheet already exists, let us redo this
Worksheets("Table of Contents").Delete
Application.DisplayAlerts = True
On Error GoTo 0

'Let us add a new worksheet as our Table of Contents
ThisWorkbook.Sheets.Add Before:=ThisWorkbook.Worksheets(1)
ActiveSheet.Name = "Table of Contents"

'Let us enumerate all of the worksheets in our ToC
For counter = 1 To Sheets.Count
'This will add one hyperlink for the specific sheet
ActiveSheet.Hyperlinks.Add _
Anchor:=ActiveSheet.Cells(counter, 1), _
Address:="", _
SubAddress:="'" & Sheets(counter).Name & "'!A1", _
ScreenTip:=Sheets(counter).Name, _
TextToDisplay:=Sheets(counter).Name

Next counter

End Sub
```

STEP 3: Let us test it out!

Open the sheet. Go to **Developer > Code > Macros**

Make sure your Macro is selected. Click **Run**.

With just one click, **a new worksheet "Table of Contents" was created**!

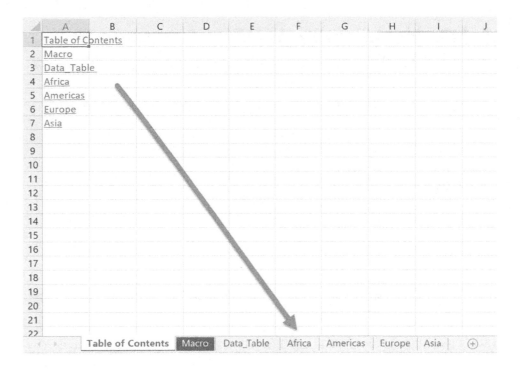

Try clicking the **Americas** link and it takes you straight to the **Americas** worksheet!

	A	B	C	D	E	F	G
1	Americas		SALES PERSON	ORDER DATE	SALES	FINANCIAL YEAR	
2			Michael Jackson	13/01/2012	$4,234.00	2012	
3			John Michaloudis	21/12/2012	$24,640.00	2012	
4			John Michaloudis	24/12/2012	$29,923.00	2012	
5			John Michaloudis	24/12/2012	$66,901.00	2012	
6			Homer Simpson	29/12/2012	$63,116.00	2012	
7			Homer Simpson	28/06/2012	$38,281.00	2012	

Table of Contents | Macro | Data_Table | Africa | **Americas** | Europe | Asia

Ready

Excel to Powerpoint

What does it do?

Copies your selected range into a new Powerpoint file

Copy Source Code:

```
'Prerequisites:
'You need to add a reference to Powerpoint Library with these
steps:
    '1. Go to Tools > References
    '2. Look for Microsoft PowerPoint 16.0 Object Library, and
check it.
    '3. Click OK
'Make sure to have a selected range before running this
Sub CopyToPowerPoint()

    Dim pptApp As PowerPoint.Application
    Dim pres As PowerPoint.Presentation
    Dim sld As PowerPoint.Slide
    Dim rng As Range

    'Copy Range from Excel
    Set rng = Selection
    rng.Copy

    'Get the Powerpoint Application
    On Error Resume Next
        Set pptApp = GetObject(, "PowerPoint.Application")
    On Error GoTo 0

    'If it does not exist yet, then open Powerpoint
    If pptApp Is Nothing Then
        Set pptApp = New PowerPoint.Application
    End If

    'Create your new presentation and setup the initial slide,
11 = ppLayoutTitleOnly
    Set pres = pptApp.Presentations.Add
    Set sld = pres.Slides.Add(1, 11)

    'Now let us paste inside the slide, 2 =
ppPasteEnhancedMetafile
```

```
    sld.Shapes.PasteSpecial DataType:=2

    pptApp.Visible = True
    pptApp.Activate
    Application.CutCopyMode = False

    Set pptApp = Nothing
    Set pres = Nothing
    Set sld = Nothing

End Sub
```

Final Result:

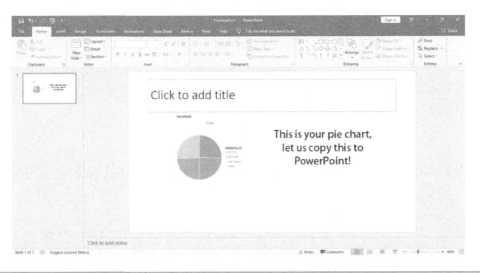

Did you know that you can use Excel Macros to copy anything from your spreadsheet into a Powerpoint presentation? Yes you can!

This is what we want to copy into a new Powerpoint file:

STEP 1: Go to *Developer* > *Code* > *Visual Basic*

Go to *Tools* > *References*

Look for **Microsoft PowerPoint 16.0 Object Library** and tick it. Click **OK.**

STEP 2: Paste in your code and **Select Save**. Close the window afterwards.

```
'Prerequisites:
'You need to add a reference to Powerpoint Library with this steps:
    '1. Go to Tools > References
    '2. Look for Microsoft PowerPoint 16.0 Object Library, and check it.
    '3. Click OK

'Make sure to have a selected range before running this
Sub CopyToPowerPoint()

    Dim pptApp As PowerPoint.Application
    Dim pres As PowerPoint.Presentation
    Dim sld As PowerPoint.Slide
    Dim rng As Range

    'Copy Range from Excel
    Set rng = Selection
    rng.Copy

    'Get the Powerpoint Application
    On Error Resume Next
        Set pptApp = GetObject(, "PowerPoint.Application")
    On Error GoTo 0

    'If it does not exist yet, then open Powerpoint
    If pptApp Is Nothing Then
        Set pptApp = New PowerPoint.Application
    End If

    'Create your new presentation and setup the initial slide, 11 = ppLayoutTitleOnly
    Set pres = pptApp.Presentations.Add
    Set sld = pres.Slides.Add(1, 11)

    'Now let us paste inside the slide, 2 = ppPasteEnhancedMetafile
    sld.Shapes.PasteSpecial DataType:=2

    pptApp.Visible = True
    pptApp.Activate
```

STEP 3: Let us test it out!

Let us pick a specific section from our spreadsheet:

Go to **Developer > Code > Macros**

Make sure your Macro is selected. Click **Run**.

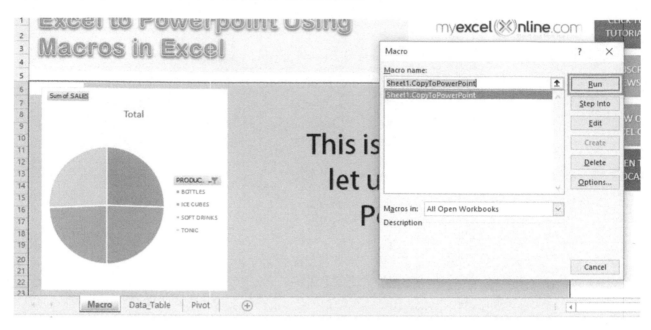

With just one click, **you now have your selected range copied into Powerpoint**!

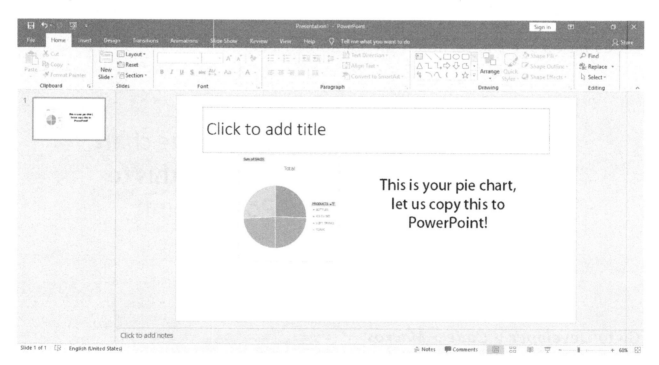

Insert a Linked Image

What does it do?

Creates a linked image based on your selection

Copy Source Code:

```
'Make sure you have a selected range first
Sub InsertALinkedImage()

Selection.Copy
'Paste the selection as an image
ActiveSheet.Pictures.Paste(Link:=True).Select

End Sub
```

Final Result:

Did you know that you can create a **linked image** in Excel?

Let us use Excel Macros to create our own **linked image**!

Let us try creating a linked image based on the MyExcelOnline logo.

(You can do this on any part of the spreadsheet, not just logos!

STEP 1: Go to *Developer > Code > Visual Basic*

STEP 2: Paste in your code and **Select Save**. Close the window afterwards.

```vba
'Make sure you have a selected range first
Sub InsertALinkedImage()

Selection.Copy
'Paste the selection as an image
ActiveSheet.Pictures.Paste(Link:=True).Select

End Sub
```

STEP 3: Let us test it out!

Open the sheet containing our target. Make sure the logo cells are highlighted.
Go to *Developer > Code > Macros*

Make sure your Macro is selected. Click **Run**.

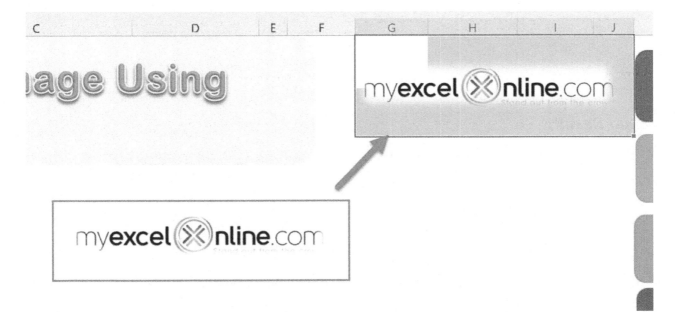

With just one click, **you have created a linked image**! Double click on it and it will highlight the logo!

Insert a Row After Each Row

What does it do?

Inserts a row after every row in your selection

Copy Source Code:

```
'Make sure you have a selection ready before running this
Sub InsertRowsAlternately()

Dim rowCnt As Integer
Dim counter As Integer

rowCnt= Selection.EntireRow.Count

For counter = 1 To rowCnt
'Insert a blank row
ActiveCell.EntireRow.Insert
'Jump to the next row
ActiveCell.Offset(2, 0).Select
Next counter

End Sub
```

Final Result:

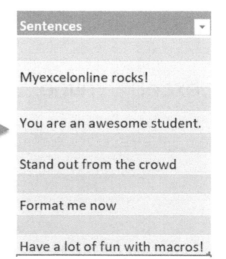

Wanted to insert alternate blank rows in your table? It's a pain to do that manually, so let us **insert a row after every row** using Excel Macros!

This is our table of data:

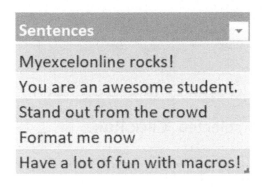

STEP 1: Go to *Developer > Code > Visual Basic*

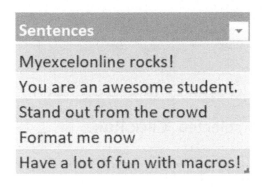

STEP 2: Paste in your code and **Select Save**. Close the window afterwards.

```vba
'Make sure you have a selection ready before running this
Sub InsertRowsAlternately()

Dim rowCount As Integer
Dim counter As Integer

rowCount = Selection.EntireRow.Count

For counter = 1 To rowCount
'Insert a blank row
ActiveCell.EntireRow.Insert
'Jump to the next row
ActiveCell.Offset(2, 0).Select
Next counter

End Sub
```

STEP 3: Let us test it out!

Open the sheet containing the data. Make sure your table is highlighted. Go to **Developer > Code > Macros**

Make sure your Macro is selected. Click **Run**.

With just one click, **you have now inserted blank rows after each row**!

Save Selected Range as PDF

What does it do?

Save selected range as a PDF file

Copy Source Code:

```
'Make sure you have something selected
Sub SaveSelectedRangeAsPdf

'The generated PDF will be opened as well
Selection.ExportAsFixedFormat Type:=xlTypePDF,
OpenAfterPublish:=True

End Sub
```

Final Result:

Excel Macros are incredibly flexible and you will be surprised with its bag of tricks! One of them is you can **save any selected range as PDF**. That's right, any section in the spreadsheet that you have selected gets saved into a PDF!

STEP 1: Go to ***Developer > Code > Visual Basic***

STEP 2: Paste in your code and **Select Save**. Close the window afterwards.

STEP 3: Let us test it out!

Let us pick a specific section from our data table:

	A	B	C	D	E	F	G	H	I	J
1	CUSTOMER	PRODUCTS	SALES PERSON	SALES REGION	ORDER DATE	SALES	FINANCIAL YEAR	SALES MONTH	SALES QTR	CHANNEL PARTNERS
2	LONG ISLANDS INC	SOFT DRINKS	Michael Jackson	AMERICAS	4/13/2012	24,640	2012	January	Q1	Acme, inc.
3	LONG ISLANDS INC	SOFT DRINKS	Michael Jackson	AMERICAS	12/21/2012	24,640	2012	February	Q1	Widget Corp
4	LONG ISLANDS INC	SOFT DRINKS	Michael Jackson	AMERICAS	12/24/2012	29,923	2012	March	Q1	123 Warehousing
5	LONG ISLANDS INC	SOFT DRINKS	Michael Jackson	AMERICAS	12/24/2012	66,901	2012	April	Q2	Demo Company
6	LONG ISLANDS INC	SOFT DRINKS	Michael Jackson	AMERICAS	12/29/2012	63,116	2012	May	Q2	Smith and Co.
7	LONG ISLANDS INC	SOFT DRINKS	Michael Jackson	AMERICAS	6/28/2012	38,281	2012	June	Q2	Foo Bars
8	LONG ISLANDS INC	SOFT DRINKS	Michael Jackson	AMERICAS	6/28/2012	57,650	2012	July	Q3	ABC Telecom
9	LONG ISLANDS INC	SOFT DRINKS	Michael Jackson	AMERICAS	6/29/2012	90,967	2012	August	Q3	Fake Brothers
10	LONG ISLANDS INC	SOFT DRINKS	Michael Jackson	AMERICAS	6/29/2012	11,910	2012	September	Q3	QWERTY Logistics
11	LONG ISLANDS INC	SOFT DRINKS	Michael Jackson	AMERICAS	7/6/2012	59,531	2012	October	Q4	Demo, inc.
12	LONG ISLANDS INC	SOFT DRINKS	Michael Jackson	AMERICAS	7/6/2012	88,297	2012	November	Q4	Sample Company
13	LONG ISLANDS INC	SOFT DRINKS	Michael Jackson	AMERICAS	9/8/2012	87,868	2012	December	Q4	Sample, inc
14	LONG ISLANDS INC	BOTTLES	Michael Jackson	AMERICAS	9/8/2012	95,527	2012	January	Q1	Acme Corp
15	LONG ISLANDS INC	BOTTLES	Michael Jackson	AMERICAS	6/30/2012	90,599	2012	February	Q1	Allied Biscuit
16	LONG ISLANDS INC	BOTTLES	Michael Jackson	AMERICAS	12/23/2012	17,030	2012	March	Q1	Ankh-Sto Associates
17	LONG ISLANDS INC	BOTTLES	Michael Jackson	AMERICAS	12/8/2012	65,026	2012	April	Q2	Extensive Enterprise
18	LONG ISLANDS INC	BOTTLES	Michael Jackson	AMERICAS	10/28/2012	57,579	2012	May	Q2	Galaxy Corp

Go to *Developer > Code > Macros*

Make sure your Macro is selected. Click **Run**.

With just one click, **you now have your selected range saved into a PDF!**

CUSTOMER	PRODUCTS	SALES PERSON	SALES REGION	ORDER DATE	SALES
LONG ISLANDS INC	SOFT DRINKS	Michael Jackson	AMERICAS	4/13/2012	24,640
LONG ISLANDS INC	SOFT DRINKS	Michael Jackson	AMERICAS	12/21/2012	24,640
LONG ISLANDS INC	SOFT DRINKS	Michael Jackson	AMERICAS	12/24/2012	29,923
LONG ISLANDS INC	SOFT DRINKS	Michael Jackson	AMERICAS	12/24/2012	66,901
LONG ISLANDS INC	SOFT DRINKS	Michael Jackson	AMERICAS	12/29/2012	63,116
LONG ISLANDS INC	SOFT DRINKS	Michael Jackson	AMERICAS	6/28/2012	38,281
LONG ISLANDS INC	SOFT DRINKS	Michael Jackson	AMERICAS	6/28/2012	57,650
LONG ISLANDS INC	SOFT DRINKS	Michael Jackson	AMERICAS	6/29/2012	90,967
LONG ISLANDS INC	SOFT DRINKS	Michael Jackson	AMERICAS	6/29/2012	11,910
LONG ISLANDS INC	SOFT DRINKS	Michael Jackson	AMERICAS	7/6/2012	59,531
LONG ISLANDS INC	SOFT DRINKS	Michael Jackson	AMERICAS	7/6/2012	88,297
LONG ISLANDS INC	SOFT DRINKS	Michael Jackson	AMERICAS	9/8/2012	87,868

Use Goal Seek

What does it do?

Executes Goal Seek in Excel

Copy Source Code:

```
'Make sure the worksheet is selected to execute the Goal Seek on
Sub GoalSeekVBA()

Dim TargetGoal As Long
'Get the target value from the user
TargetGoal = InputBox("Enter the target value", "Enter Goal")

'Make sure to change the cell that you want to be changed with
the goal
ActiveSheet.Range("E9").GoalSeek _
    Goal:=TargetGoal, _
    ChangingCell:=Range("A9")
End Sub
```

Final Result:

	A	B	C	D	E
7					
8	INITIAL AMOUNT	INTEREST RATE	NUMBER OF YEARS	MONTHLY	TOTAL
9	$ 68,921.35	4%	10	$ 1,000.00	$250,000.00

Ever heard of the **Goal Seek** feature in Excel? It is a very nice feature where it takes out the guesswork for you and determines the input value needed to achieve a specific goal. For example, you have a goal / result in mind, but you are unsure what the starting amount should be for an investment. Let us use Excel Macros to execute the **Goal Seek feature!**

This is our scenario. We have a formula calculating our target goal:

- The initial amount is $5000
- Interest rate is 4%
- Number of years is 10
- Monthly additional investment is $1000
- With these parameters, after 10 years, your investment will be equivalent to $154,703.97

F9		:	×	✓	f_x	=FV(B9/12,C9*12,D9,A9)*-1	

	A	B	C	D	E
7					
8	INITIAL AMOUNT	INTEREST RATE	NUMBER OF YEARS	MONTHLY	TOTAL
9	$ 5,000.00	4%	10	$ 1,000.00	$154,703.97
10					
11					

Let us now assume that, given we want to achieve **a goal of $250,000**. What will our initial amount be?

Take note of the following:

- Initial Amount - Cell A9
- Total Amount (Goal) - Cell E9

STEP 1: Go to *Developer > Code > Visual Basic*

STEP 2: Paste in your code and **Select Save**. Close the window afterwards.

Do take note that we are referencing these two cells in the code:

- Initial Amount - Cell A9
- Total Amount (Goal) - Cell E9

What goal seek will do, is it will adjust the initial amount (Cell A9), to achieve the target goal that you specify (Cell E9) which is $250,000.

STEP 3: Let us test it out!

Open the sheet containing the data. Go to **Developer > Code > Macros**

Make sure your Macro is selected. Click **Run**.

Type in the target value of $250,000. See how the initial amount will change.

	A	B	C	D	E	F
7						
8	INITIAL AMOUNT	INTEREST RATE	NUMBER OF YEARS	MONTHLY	TOTAL	
9	$ 5,000.00	4%	10	$ 1,000.00	$154,703.97	
10						

Enter Goal ✕

Enter the target value

250000

OK

Cancel

With just one click, **Goal Seek computed that you need an initial amount of $68,921.35 to achieve your goal of $250,000!**

	A	B	C	D	E
7					
8	INITIAL AMOUNT	INTEREST RATE	NUMBER OF YEARS	MONTHLY	TOTAL
9	$ 68,921.35	4%	10	$ 1,000.00	$250,000.00

Use the Data Entry Form

What does it do?

Loads the data form to allow you to populate data to the table

Copy Source Code:

```
Sub UseDataEntryForm()
'Show the default data entry form
ActiveSheet.ShowDataForm
End Sub
```

Final Result:

Have a lot of details to encode in your table? You can use Excel Macros to open the **data entry form** for you with one click!

This is our table that we want to populate data on:

Name	Address	Phone Number	

STEP 1: Go to **_Developer_** > **_Code_** > **_Visual Basic_**

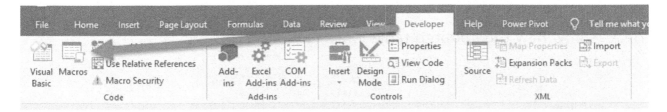

STEP 2: Paste in your code and **Select Save**. Close the window afterwards.

```
Sub UseDataEntryForm()

    'Show the default data entry form
    ActiveSheet.ShowDataForm

End Sub
```

STEP 3: Let us test it out!

Open the sheet containing the data. Make sure the correct sheet is selected. Go to **_Developer_** > **_Code_** > **_Macros_**

Make sure your Macro is selected. Click **Run**.

With just one click, **you now have the data form loaded up**! Let us try populating a couple of records then click **Close**.

Here is now how the updated table looks like!

	A	B	C	D
1	Name	Address	Phone Number	
2	John	MyExcelOnline HQ	12345	
3	John Doe	New York	54321	
4	Bryan	MyExcelOnline HQ	11111	
5				
6				
7				

MYEXCELONLINE ACADEMY COURSE

We are offering you access to our online Excel membership course – The MyExcelOnline Academy – **for only $1 for the first 30 days!**

Copy & Paste this $1 Trial URL to your web browser to get access to this special reader offer:

👉 https://www.myexcelonline.com/$1trial

Here is the **download link** that has all the workbooks covered in this book (copy & paste this URL to your web browser):

👉 https://www.myexcelonline.com/macros-download

Made in the USA
Las Vegas, NV
10 January 2022

40988855R00201